BUDGERIGAR HANDBOOK

by

ERNEST H. HART

line drawings by the author

●

istributed in the U.S. by T.F.H. Publications, Inc., 211 West Sylvania venue, P.O. Box 427, Neptune, N.J. 07753; in England by T.F.H. (Gt. ritain) Ltd., 13 Nutley Lane, Reigate, Surrey; in Canada to the book tore and library trade by Clarke, Irwin & Company, Clarwin House, 791 t. Clair Avenue West, Toronto 10, Ontario; in Canada to the pet trade y Rolf C. Hagen Ltd., 3225 Sartelon Street, Montreal 382, Quebec; in outheast Asia by Y.W. Ong, 9 Lorong 36 Geylang, Singapore 14; in ustralia and the South Pacific by Pet Imports Pty. Ltd., P.O. Box 149, rookvale 2100, N.S.W., Australia; in South Africa by Valiant ublishers (Pty.) Ltd., P.O. Box 78236, Sandton City, 2146, South frica; Published by T.F.H. Publications, Inc., Ltd., The British Crown olony of Hong Kong.

ISBN 0-87666-414-1

CONTENTS

To

the author's chicks

Lynn, Lance, and Keith

FOREWORD

This book has been expressly written for the breeder of Budgerigars who earnestly wishes to improve his stock through the application of tested and approved knowledge not hitherto readily available. Whether you breed for show stock or to supply the pet market, you will find in these pages information that will bring greater success and more pleasure to your hobby.

Essentially the breeding of exhibition Budgerigars is both a science and an art; to attain consistent success one must take complete advantage of all the knowledge, experience, and research accumulated in this and allied fields. For centuries the breeding of animals was the result of shrewd guessing by the breeder, combined with an innate "feel" in the selection of breeding partners. But this system of selection has changed, for never before has man placed so much trust in learning as in our time, and this is as it should be if he is to keep pace with the forward surge of modern knowledge.

Advances in agriculture and animal husbandry have been rapid and astounding in recent years. But, in the pet or hobby field there have been no great steps forward, simply because research has been concentrated in the economic field of animal and plant production for human consumption. Yet we who breed Budgies can find much that is useful in the findings of research in these parallel fields and, by testing and experimentation, adapt it to our own use.

The author has spent several years of research in Budgerigar genetics, husbandry and nutrition. To these findings have been added the experience and intelligent perception of recognized authorities, plus knowledge gleaned from other fields and tested in the author's aviaries to weigh its worth. In this book you will find the sum of this research and knowledge presented in an orderly, easily understood fashion so that it can be employed by the reader in his own aviary.

big, bold, steady-on-the-perch, exhibition quality Grey ormal hen bred in Britain, the kind of quality dam that produces winners when used correctly.

The author wishes to express his thanks to Dominick Golia, Jr., for his fine photographs, and for his ready cooperation during the preparation of this book. Many of the superb Budgerigars seen on these pages are his, and some of Mr. Golia's valuable stock from his winning strains of imported birds were made available to the author for his experiments.

For the past several years I have traveled extensively and spent some time viewing Budgies in aviaries and shows in the British Isles and Germany specifically and in other countries generally. In the two mentioned continental areas, and particularly in the British Isles, the colorful immigrant from Australia has reached, in the hands of the better and more knowledgeable breeders, an almost unbelievable strata of perfection. Of course I also studied their methods of feeding, husbandry and breeding. In this revised edition of the Budgerigar Handbook you will find fine photographs of many of the continental birds. Today, in the author's aviaries, are birds from a few of these Scotch and English sources, including Collyer, Bryan, Kirby-Mason and Dabner, Miller, Fulgoni, McCleary and North. Some of this stock also comes from my very good friends, Francis Curran (McCleary, Miller, and Bryan), Tony Mancini, and William Hagymasy (North and Fulgoni), as well as new and valuable stock of imported breeding (Miller and McCleary) from Dom Golia.

If, through one sentence, page, paragraph or chapter, you who read this book can glean some worth which will enable you to better use the living tools with which you are working, and so find more satisfaction and success in your hobby, then the purpose for which this book was conceived has been achieved.

ERNEST H. HART

BUDGERIGAR HANDBOOK

Wide in the brow, with a small, tucked-in beak and large, well-spaced spots. The brow of this excellent Normal Green hen overhangs her eyes, a desirable feature. This is a truly typey, exhibition hen of undeniable worth as a show bird or breeder. As seen in the photograph the only feature in which we would like to see improvement is in greater depth of the bib area. This Budgie was bred and exhibited in Germany and is an example of the best that German breeders have attained.

Chapter 1
FORMING A STUD

The budgerigar, or green grass parakeet, is a warm-blooded, vertebrate animal of the class, *Aves*. The scientific name for this most interesting bird is *Melopsittacus undulatus*. In Australia, its native habitat, great flocks of wild, green budgies migrate periodically from one district to another in search of the ripe grass seeds which form their staple diet. They nest in gum trees, rotting logs or tree trunks, scooping out their nests with their strong, hooked beaks and raising a clutch of, on the average, six chicks.

From these basic wild parakeets the modern domesticated budgerigar was evolved. Through the efforts of earnest breeders, principally in England where the budgerigar has been bred for almost eighty years and has been brought to its highest state of refinement in modern times, a huge fancy has been built which now embraces all continents. Budgerigar societies have been formed, standards have been set and the little native of Australia has now become the most popular cage and exhibition bird in the world.

As a pet the budgie is without peer. As a show bird he is magnificent in his many colored garments, and the very difficulties inevitably associated with the breeding of exhibition stock to a specific standard of conformation recommends him to the earnest breeder and hobbyist.

We begin the approach to any endeavor as a novice, and the novice budgie enthusiast is generally attracted to this easily bred species by its myriad color mutations. Next, the novice becomes fascinated by the rare color and pattern combinations he can create in his own breeding room. He has little knowledge of the true exhibition type and, in many cases, does not know that there exists a recognized budgerigar standard of perfection. He breeds his birds, learns how to care for them and feed them, in a superficial manner, sees reproduction take place and, by this mere multiplication of a species, considers himself a breeder. Eventually, he becomes aware of the fact that there are books about budgies and that there are bird shows where budgerigars are exhibited. Through these media he learns about his local Budgerigar Society and becomes a member and, eventually becomes conscious of type. But his former efforts have not been wasted, for through them he has served a valuable apprenticeship and he is now ready to enter into a much more serious phase which will bring him greater satisfaction, and fulfilment to his hobby.

Once the neophyte discovers there is more to breeding than mere production he becomes avid of new knowledge. He should definitely join any local society, for there he will meet people with similar interests. Among them he will find earnest exhibition breeders who own and breed fine show type birds and from them he can purchase stock that will set him on the road to success.

WHERE TO PURCHASE STOCK

Top winning show birds of excellent breeding can seldom be purchased, even when they can, the price will be so formidable as to be prohibitive. The author recently wrote to a winning stud in England to purchase a pair of top, young birds and the price quoted was £1,000 which, at the present rate of exchange, is equal to $2,800. But, secondary birds of fine breeding, not quite up to exhibition standards, can be bought for a nominal price and, if judiciously used, produce stock equal to, and sometimes surpassing, the stock produced by their more true-to-type relatives. The average price for such young stock, which carry fifty percent or more English breeding, ranges from about $35 upward.

It is wiser to buy the well-bred culls produced by a consistently winning family from a successful exhibition breeder, than the best birds from an aviary that has never produced an outstanding bird. The knowledgeable breeder of exhibition budgerigars frequently advances so steadily each year that the birds he doesn't want and will sell to you this year are, in type and worth, equal to the budgies he thought good enough to keep for his own breeding last year.

SELECTION OF BASIC STOCK

Purchase as many pairs of this good stock (within reason) as your pocketbook allows. Four pairs will be a good start. In your selection confine yourself to one, or at the most, two series of colors so that the resulting stock from your purchased pairs can

A cinnamon, section-winning hen of Scottish and English ancestory. This bird is
a light green cinnamon.

be interbred without complication. While selecting this basic stock visualize "type" as depicted by the "standard" as ideal. Remember the winning birds you saw at the shows and recall the reasons why they were superior to the other exhibits. Reach back into memory and find the answers you received to the many questions you asked of breeders and judges when you made a pest of yourself at numerous shows, aviaries and club meetings in your search for knowledge and so learned and absorbed much valuable information. Apply all this that you know to your purchase of stock but, not aloud and in an authoritative mien or the breeder to whom you have come to purchase these birds will give you no help. Instead be humble, listen to the breeder, take his advice for he knows his birds better than you do and, in most cases, he will earnestly attempt to sell you stock that will aid you to reach your goal.

Select your hens as much as possible, for width of head, as seen from the front, good backskull, substance, size and good position on the perch. The cocks should have type, good markings and color. They should be good in frontal, topskull, depth of bib and show spots as large and round as possible. If the necklace spots are not too large, be sure then that they are even and of like size. This particularly pertains to the inside spots which should not be smaller than the outer spots, a difficult fault to breed out.

If you have owned and bred budgies previous to your purchase of the good stock, do not immediately get rid of your former scrub stock. Keep those pairs in equal number to your good pairs which have proved in previous seasons to be good feeders, keeping their chicks crop-filled and content, and not given to nest box vices such as feather picking, savaging the young or wet feeding. Be sure that none of the pairs you keep for feeders have ever produced French moulters. Good feeder pairs can prove to be invaluable as foster parents to the young of your more valuable birds and allow you to produce much more stock to select from your show-bred birds. You will find the foster parent method discussed in full detail in Chapter 4.

It is essential to have all the good qualities you wish to establish in your strain in your initial breeding stock. These properties can be either dominant, that is, visible in the individuals, or carried in a hidden or recessive state. In the latter case one must be sure that the family, especially the close relatives of the bird, exhibit the wanted virtues or, in the case of proven breeding pairs, that they have transmitted these qualities to a reasonable proportion of their progeny. By proper mating then, those desired properties which are hidden or recessive in the parents can yet be passed on to a percentage of their young in visible form. These good qualities or wanted virtues can then be blended and concentrated in future breeding seasons by proper breeding procedures. Remember that you cannot put into the progeny anything more than the parents themselves possess either visible or hidden, dominant or recessive.

SELECTION OF BREEDING PAIRS

When selecting the individuals for your breeding teams never mate a pair which, as individuals, exhibit the same fault or faults. First evaluate each cock and hen separately and breed the best cock to the best hen, the second best cock to the second best hen, and so on, remembering to be careful not to mate fault to fault as mentioned above. You may find that your second, third or fourth choice pair produce better chicks than your first choice pair. If certain pairs do not produce well together break up the pair, put the cock to another hen and the hen to a different cock. In this way, and with only four basic pairs, various new breeding combinations can be tried.

It now becomes apparent why it is advisedly best to limit your stock to one, or at the most two color series which, when interbred, produce no color or modifier complications. If, for example, you select a violet split cinnamon cock to breed to a sky hen they will produce sky, sky violet (which you would probably be unable to differentiate from cobalt), cobalt and violet. You would also get a small percentage of cinnamon hens. If it was your purpose to select for violet and/or cinnamon your choice would be extremely limited since the percentages of these varieties from the above mating would be small. None might appear in the first nest at all and, if they did, you would be selecting for limited color variety alone instead of for the type improvements which would upgrade your stud, and so you defeat your own purpose. If, on the other hand, you were to breed sky to sky, all the progeny would be sky and you would have no problem in selecting the chicks that exhibit the wanted improvements.

COLOR VARIETIES

It would perhaps be wise at this time to list the visual color varieties as recognized and interpreted by the Budgerigar Society so that the reader can fairly accurately visualize the various varieties.

For general reference, regardless of what the color may be, all color in all varieties should be bright and even or level. Patchiness is undesirable and should be exhibited only by birds in a moult. The color of a healthy, adult budgerigar in prime condition should show sheen and bloom. Some normal birds, particularly males, through the neck, back and wings show a brilliant wash of the body color that tints the white feather edges in a fashion similar to the opaline. This lustre gives even greater beauty to the bird and is highly desirable.

Hens are generally slightly duller in overall color than cocks. The listing which follows applies only to adult exhibition budgerigars in top condition.

COLOR STANDARDS
By courtesy of The Budgerigar Society (England)

Light Green.—Mask: Buttercup of an even tone ornamented on each side of throat with three clearly defined black spots, one of which appears at the base of the cheek patch. Cheek Patches: Violet. General Body Color: Back, rump, breast, flanks, and underparts, bright grass-green of a solid and even shade throughout; markings on cheeks, back of head, neck and wings, black and well-defined on a buttercup ground. Tail: Long feathers blue-black.

Dark Green.—As above but of a dark laurel-green body color. Tail: Long feathers darker in proportion.

Olive Green.—As above but of a deep olive-green body color. Tail: Long feathers darker in proportion.

Light Yellow (including Cinnamon Light Yellow).—Mask: Buttercup; back, rump, breast, flanks, wings, and underparts, buttercup and as free from green suffusion as possible; primaries lighter than body. Tail: Long feathers lighter than body color.

Dark Yellow (including Cinnamon Dark Yellow).—As above but of a deeper body color.

Olive Yellow (including Cinnamon Olive Yellow).—As above but of a mustard body color.

16

A nice graywing hen.

Skyblue.—Mask: Clear white ornamented on each side of throat with three clearly defined black spots, one of which appears at the base of the cheek patch. Cheek Patches: Violet. General Body Color: Back, rump, breast, flanks, and underparts, pure skyblue; markings on cheeks, back of head, neck, and wing, black and well-defined on a white ground. Tail: Long feathers blue-black.

Cobalt.—As above, but of a rich deep cobalt-blue body color. Tail: Long feathers darker in proportion.

Mauve.—As above, but body color purplish mauve, with a tendency to a pinkish tone. Tail: Long feathers darker in proportion.

Violet.—As Skyblue but of a deep intense violet body color. Tail: Long feathers darker in proportion.

Whites (including Cinnamon Whites) of Light Suffusion. —Mask: White. General Body Color: Back, rump, breast, flanks, and underparts, white, wings and tail pure white.

NOTE.—The only difference in the various varieties of white is in the cheek patches, which in every case are a pale color of the variety they represent.

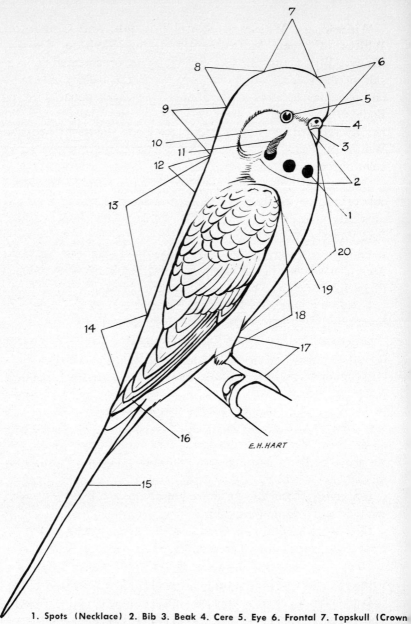

E.H.HART

1. Spots (Necklace) 2. Bib 3. Beak 4. Cere 5. Eye 6. Frontal 7. Topskull (Crown
8. Backskull 9. Neck 10. Cheek 11. Cheek Patch 12. Withers 13. Back Prope
14. Rump 15. Tail 16. Flights 17. Legs and Feet 18. Wing 19. Shoulder 20. Front Line

Whitewings, Whites of Deep Suffusion, and Cinnamon Whites of Deep Suffusion (including Skyblue, Cobalt, Mauve, Violet and Grey).—Mask: White, ornamented on each side of the throat with three grey spots (the paler the better), one of which appears at the base of the cheek patch. General Body Color: Back, rump, breast, flanks, and underparts, very heavily suffused body color approximating to the normal variety. Wings and Tail: Pure white. Cheek Patches: In every case a pale color of the variety they represent.

Greywing Light Green.—Mask: Yellow, ornamented each side of throat with three clearly defined spots of smoky grey, one of which appears at the base of the cheek patch. Cheek Patches: Pale Violet. General Body Color: Back, rump, breast, flanks, and underparts, pale grass-green. Markings on cheeks, back of head, neck, and wings, should be smoky grey, half-way between black and zero. Tail: Long feathers smoky grey with pale bluish tinge.

Greywing Dark Green.—As above but of a light laurel-green body color. Tail: Long feathers darker in proportion.

Greywing Olive Green.—As above but of a light olive-green body color. Tail: Long feathers darker still in proportion.

Greywing Skyblue.—Mask: White, ornamented each side of throat with three clearly defined grey spots, one of which appears at the base of the cheek patch. Cheek Patches: Light Violet. General Body Color: Back, rump, breast, flanks, and underparts, clear pale skyblue. Markings: on cheeks, back of head, neck, and wings: pure grey, halfway between black and zero. Tail: Long feathers greyish blue.

Greywing Cobalt.—As above but of a pale cobalt body color, with tail of corresponding color.

Greywing Violet.—As Greywing Skyblue, but of a pale violet body color, with tail of corresponding color.

Greywing Mauve.—As above but of a pale mauve body color, with tail of corresponding color.

Greywing Grey Green.—As Greywing Light Green but with body color of light mustard green. Cheek Patches: Light grey. Tail: Long tail feathers deep grey.

Greywing Grey.—As Greywing Skyblue but with body color of pale grey. Cheek Patches: Pale grey. Tail: Feathers deep grey.

Cinnamon Light Green.—Mask: Yellow, ornamented on each side of throat with three clearly-defined cinnamon-brown spots, one of which appears at the base of the cheek patch. Cheek Patches: Violet. General Body Color: Back, rump, breast, flanks, and underparts, pale grass-green. Markings on cheeks, back of head, neck, and wings: cinnamon-brown well-defined on a yellow ground. Tail: Long feathers dark blue with brown quill.

Cinnamon Dark Green.—As above, but of a light laurel-green body color. Tail: Long feathers darker in proportion.

Cinnamon Olive Green.—As above, but with a light olive-green body color. Tail: Long feathers darker in proportion.

Cinnamon Skyblue.—Mask: White ornamented on each side of throat with three clearly defined cinnamon-brown spots, one of which appears at the base of the cheek patch. Cheek Patches: Violet. General Body Color: Back, rump, breast, flanks, and underparts, pale sky-blue. Markings on cheeks, back of head, neck, and wings: cinnamon brown on white ground. Tail: Long feathers blue with brown quill.

Cinnamon Cobalt.—As above, but with general body color of pale cobalt. Tail: Long feathers as above, but cobalt.

Cinnamon Mauve.—As above, but with general body color of pale mauve. Tail: Long feathers as above, but mauve.

Cinnamon Grey.—As Cinnamon Skyblue but with body color of pale grey. Tail: Long feathers of deep cinnamon shade.

Cinnamon Grey Green.—As Cinnamon Light Green but with body color of pale grey. Tail: Long tail feathers of deep cinnamon shade.

Cinnamon Violet.—As Cinnamon Skyblue but with general body color of pale violet. Tail: Long tail feathers of pale cinnamon shade.

NOTE.—In all forms of Cinnamon the male bird carries a deeper shade than the female.

Fallow Light Green.—Mask: Yellow, ornamented on each side of throat with three clearly defined brown spots, one of which appears at the base of the cheek patch. Cheek Patches: Violet. General Body Color: Back, rump, breast, flanks, and underparts, yellowish green. Markings on cheeks, back of head, neck, and wings: dark brown on a yellow ground. Eyes: Clear red or plum. Tail: Long feathers bluish grey.

An exhibition English cock of excellent substance and quality. Note the roundness of the skull, the perfect bib depth and spots, the desirable front and back lines. The bird stands well up on the perch and leaves litle to be wanted in an exhibition Budgerigar. This Budgie has won many top honors in English shows.

Depth of bib and beautifully spaced, large, round spots catch
the eye immediately when viewing this exhibition Budgie. The
beak is partly open destroying the tucked-in, tight look in
this area that the bird actually possesses. The skull is quite
wide and seems to lack frontal rise, but this latter look is
caused by the camera angle, shooting upward instead of
head-on. This good English bird evidently has very desirable
substance and stance.

Fallow Dark Green.—As above, but with pale laurel-green body color. Tail: Long feathers darker in proportion.

Fallow Olive Green.—As above, but with light mustard-olive body color. Tail: Long feathers darker in proportion.

Fallow Skyblue.—Mask: White, ornamented on each side of throat with three clearly defined brown spots, one of which appears at the base of the cheek patch. Cheek Patches: Violet. General Body Color: Back, rump, breast, flanks, and underparts, pale skyblue. Markings on cheek, back of head, neck, and wings: dark brown on a white ground. Eyes: Clear red or plum. Tail: Long feathers bluish-grey.

Fallow Cobalt.—As above, but with a warm cobalt body color. Tail: Long feathers darker in proportion.

Fallow Mauve.—As above, but with a pale mauve body color of pinkish tone. Tail: Long feathers darker in proportion.

Fallow Violet.—As Fallow Skyblue but with a pale violet body. Tail: Long tail feathers darker in proportion.

Light Forms.—The Committee recognises the existence of a light form of Cinnamon and Fallow identical to the normal already described, but lighter in body color and markings.

Pure Yellow Red-Eyes (Lutinos).—Buttercup throughout. Eyes: Clear red. Tail: Long feathers and primaries greyish-white.

Pure White Red-Eyes (Albinos).—White throughout. Eyes: Clear red.

Yellow Wing Light Green.—Mask: Buttercup, ornamented on each side of throat with three smoky-grey spots (the paler the better), one of which appears at the base of the cheek patch. General Body Color: Back, rump, breast, flanks, and underparts, bright grass-green. Wings: Buttercup. Tail: Long feathers pale grass-green.

Yellow Wing Dark Green.—As above, but with general body color of laurel-green; long tail feathers darker in proportion.

Yellow Wing Olive Green.—As above, but with general body color of olive green. Tail: Long feathers darker in proportion.

Opaline Light Green.—Mask: Buttercup yellow, extending over back of head and merging into general body color at a point level with the butt of wings, where undulations should cease, thus leaving a clear "V" effect between top of wings so desirable in this variety; mask to be ornamented by six large black throat spots, the outer two being partially covered at the base of violet cheek patches. General Body Color: Mantle (including "V" area or saddle), back, rump, breast, flanks, and underparts, bright grass-green. Wings: To be iridescent and of the same color as body; markings should be normal and symmetrical; long tail feathers not to be lighter than mantle.

Opaline Dark Green.—As above, but of a dark laurel-green body color. Tail: Long feathers darker in proportion.

Opaline Olive Green.—As above, but of an olive-green body color. Tail: Long feathers darker in proportion.

Opaline Skyblue.—As above, but with a skyblue body color and suffusion, and white mask instead of buttercup. Tail: Long feathers not to be lighter than mantle.

Opaline Cobalt.—As Skyblue, but of a cobalt body color. Tail: Long feathers darker in proportion.

Opaline Mauve.—As Skyblue, but of a mauve body color. Tail: Long tail feathers deeper in proportion.

Opaline Violet.—As Opaline Skyblue but of a deep intense violet body color. Tail: Long feathers not to be darker than mantle.

Opaline Grey.—As Opaline Skyblue but with body color of solid grey. Tail: Long tail feathers to be not lighter than mantle, cheek patches of grey.

Opaline Grey Green.—As Opaline Light Green but with body color of dull mustard green. Tail: Long tail feathers not to be lighter than mantle, cheek patches of grey.

Yellow Face.—Mask only: Yellow, otherwise exactly as corresponding normal variety.

NOTE.—Yellow-marked feathers in tail permissible.

Grey.—Mask: White, ornamented on each side of throat with three clearly defined black spots, one of which appears at the base of the cheek patch. Cheek Patches: Grey. General Body Color: Back, rump, breast, flanks, and underparts, solid grey. Markings on cheeks, back of head, neck and wings: Black and well-defined of a white ground. Tail: Long feathers black.

NOTE.—The terms Light, Medium and Dark, describe the skyblue, cobalt and mauve forms respectively.

Light Grey Green.—This variety conforms to the standard for light green except in the following details: Cheek Patches:

Head study of a great green cock. This bird won Best-in-Show many times. Note the width of skull, depth of bib and size of spots.

Grey. General Body Color: Dull mustard green. Tail: Long feathers black.

Medium Grey Green.—This term denotes the dark-green form of the grey.

Dark Grey Green.—This form represents the grey olive-green.

NOTE.—The Committee do not feel justified at this juncture in describing Medium Grey Green and Dark Grey Green. As soon as enough data are available detailed descriptions will be published.

Slate.—Mask: White, ornamented on each side of throat with three clearly defined black spots, one of which appears at the base of the cheek patch. Cheek Patches: Violet. General Body Color: Back, rump, breast, flanks, and underparts, even greenish slate. Markings on cheeks, back of head, neck and wing: black and well defined on a white ground. Tail: Long feathers blue-black.

NOTE.—The terms Light, Medium and Dark, describe the skyblue cobalt and mauve form respectively.

Light Slate Green.—In every respect as the standard for light green, except that the general body color is sage green.

NOTE.—The terms Light, Medium and Dark describe the light green, dark green, and olive forms respectively.

COLOR BREEDING

Here you will again find a listing of color varieties but, in this instance the purpose is to indicate how best these colors and varieties may be produced. You will discover which basic breedings will produce the best color with retention of type in the various color categories.

Mention must be made here of texture since it accompanies the wanted sheen in color. A budgerigar with coarse plumage cannot display its color to full advantage, presenting a ragged and unkempt appearance. It is a known fact that the cinnamon phase possesses silky, fine, feather texture as does also the Australian grey. Both transmit this quality to stock lines which carry their breeding, even as a recessive (in the case of the cinnamon), where the factor is not visible.

The light green is the true budgerigar color and all other colors, patterns, and varieties are the result of mutations. Basically, all budgerigars can be classified in two color groups, green and blue. These two groups are divided into different intensities and shades by modifiers, but all are either green or blue genetically.

There are numerous breedings other than those mentioned that will produce the desired colors and, in many instances, will get superior stock. The measure of success lies in the results obtained, not in the formula. Regardless of what breeding pairs you employ to produce the desired colors, they must themselves and through their genetic heritage, be rich and deep in color and, aside from color, be capable of bringing advancement in type to their progeny.

To further clarify color and variety breeding, reference should be made to Chapter 10, where sex-linkage and the effect of the various modifiers are explained and charted for easy reference.

LIGHT GREEN

The green color in budgerigars is dominant to all other colors. Breed a pure green to any other color and the chicks resulting from the mating will be green in color, but split (carrying a recessive) to produce the partner color when mated to a bird of the partner series.* The only colors that can effect the green are the Australian grey and the violet. Even then the resulting bird is still green though the color has been modified, not changed. The exhibition light green seems to hold closer to type, have a better head, spots, and larger size than the other colors on the average, perhaps because they possess the basic breed color from which all other colors and shades have departed as mutations. Also, improvements are easier to fix and hold in the dominant green series. Many breeders use top light greens to bring improvement in type and size to other colors. This is termed, by the British, as "Dipping into the Green." Though this procedure is still advocated, the author believes that it is, in most instances, no longer necessary. Most of the basic colors in normal and opaline have reached a point of development in the past few years where they need only selection within their own color sphere to effect improvement.

*A split is indicated by the slanted dividing line as in green/blue (green split blue) and indicates that, though the bird is a visual green it carries a recessive, or hidden factor, for blue and, if bred to a bird of the recessive color series, will produce a percentage of the recessive color progeny which will be pure for that color. A budgerigar can only be split to a recessive character, never to a dominant.

Light green × light green is a good mating if your desire is to produce a line of good light greens. Be careful of feather texture in the bigger birds. If improvement in texture is necessary a cross to the Type I light Australian grey will help and you will also produce the lovely grey green. Be sure the grey used is a one-factor bird, so that you will produce 50 percent of each color, light green and grey green.

If improvement in any particular feature is necessary which cannot be furnished by any pure green, select a good green/sky blue or an opaline in light green, green/blue or grey if they are strong in the needed improvement. With these matings you will produce enough light greens in the nest to indulge in selection.

DARK GREEN

To produce dark greens, a one-factor bird (see Chapter 10) light green × olive is the best mating since this breeding will give you all dark greens. Good olives though, are difficult to find. Light green × mauve will also produce all dark greens, but they will be split to blue and will be valuable in the production of cobalts. If your basic stock is in the green and blue series light green × cobalt will give you approximately 50 percent dark green blue (type II) which, when bred to your blue series, will produce a Mendelian ratio of 50 percent blue and 50 percent green. These same greens/blue bred into your green stock will produce all greens of which 50 percent will be split to blue.

OLIVE GREEN

Olive × mauve, which will produce all olives but split to blue, is considered by most authorities to be the best mating for the production of this two-dark-factor shade. If two good, big olives can be found and bred, pure olives will be the result. A good cobalt, generally superior in type than the olive, if of good deep, even color, can be used as one of the partners, olive × cobalt. The resulting 50 percent olive/blue young should be well worthwhile and can also be used in the production of good mauves.

LIGHT YELLOW (Pastel Green)

The exhibition light yellow must show depth and purity of color with no evidence of green suffusion. To produce this purity the mating light yellow × light yellow is best. It is genetically a pastel mutation of the green and recessive to true green intensity. The color tends to vary in shade from buff to true, pure yellow.

Dark yellows and olive yellows are seldom bred for exhibition purposes and serve little purpose in the stud.

SKY BLUE

This attractive color can best be produced by the mating skyblue × skyblue which will produce 100 percent skyblue youngsters. Many breeders claim that this mating, generation after generation, will eventually result in a faded, washed-out sky color and a diminishing of size in the series. They advocate "Dipping into the Green" to keep size and color intensity. But if good, large, typical stock is used possessing a heritage of deep clear color density, and constant selection is made for size and true color, these attributes can be maintained in your stud without the introduction of green to your skyblue line.

If, due to hidden recessives in your stock, size and color *do* degenerate, then it is time to introduce green. Under these circumstances dark green/blue × skyblue, if the dark green shows the desired improvements, is a good breeding.

COBALT

A typical cobalt of good color is difficult to produce. One reason is because the cobalt possesses the partially dominant dark factor in single dose. When two cobalts are bred together only half of the progeny are cobalts, the other 50 percent is divided equally between sky (no dark factor) and mauve (two dark factors). To produce the most and perhaps the best cobalts, the mating sky × mauve is recommended. From this mating, only cobalts will be produced, giving you greater latitude in selection for improvement. The cobalt color varies greatly in shade and density even among brothers and sisters in the same nest.

MAUVE

Olive/blue, the recessive blue having been a good, deep mauve, not cobalt, bred to mauve (mauve × olive/blue) seems to produce the best mauves, along with some good olive/blues. If you have a pair of good, deep colored mauves of the desired color and type, they can be bred together to produce 100 percent mauve offspring. A good violet mauve × cobalt can also produce excellent level-shade mauves, if the cobalt employed is of an even rich color.

VIOLET

The violet is a cobalt to which, by mutation, a pink wash has been added to the basic cobalt color. The genetic formula of this variety is rather complex. It is best for the breeder who wishes to produce violets to consider it a cobalt and in his matings employ the breeding techniques he would to produce cobalts. Like the cobalt, the violet is a one-dark-factor bird but, unlike the cobalt, the violet possesses color penetration modifiers. A violet carrying one color penetration modifier exhibits partial dominance. Two of these modifiers result in complete dominance (*see* Chapter 10). There is no outward difference between the violet carrier of one or two modifiers; and since few birds possessing the modifier in double form are in existence, it is best to consider all violets as of the single-modifier class.

The violet can be bred in the visual form, true violet, and in two so-called non-visual forms, sky violet and mauve violet. The sky violet looks very much like a cobalt and the mauve violet generally has the appearance of any other mauve. In most cases the true color characteristics of the sky violet (a no-dark-factor bird) and the mauve violet (a two-dark-factor bird) can only be ascertained by breeding results. It is therefore best for the breeder to use a visual violet as one member of his violet-producing breeding team.

In any breeding where the visual violet is used, violet × sky, violet × cobalt, violet × mauve, 50 percent of the offspring will be cobalt, and half of these cobalts will be visual violet. Violet × sky and violet × cobalt will also produce a percentage of sky violets. Violet × cobalt and violet × mauve will throw some mauve violets. If, by the progeny test, a sky and/or a mauve prove to possess the violet factor, the mating of sky × mauve, with one or both of the partners carrying the violet factor, will produce more visual violets than any other mating.

The violet factor in the green series is again difficult to ascertain unless one has had experience with this color form. To avoid further complication it is best to confine violet matings within the structure of the blue series.

AUSTRALIAN GREY

There have been several grey mutations in the blue series, but the one which has survived is the dominant Australian grey. This color (or lack of color) can be bred in three shades corresponding in depth to the sky, cobalt, and mauve in the blue series birds. The lightest (no dark factor) grey is the most attractive.

This color is dominant to blue and works as a modifier in the green series. Being dominant, the color can be reproduced in the first generation. Like the violet, the Australian grey possesses both the color intensity modifiers and the color penetration modifiers. If it carries one penetration modifier, it exhibits partial dominance and 50 percent of the young will be greys. If it is a double-penetration modifier bird, it shows complete dominance and can produce 100 percent grey poults.

Grey bred to green modifies the basic green color and produces the lovely grey green. The Australian grey is generally a typy bird and can bring improvement in type and feather texture to your stock. To produce light grey, breed a grey to a sky. Medium, dark as well as light grey, can be produced by the mating grey × cobalt. Medium and dark grey by breeding grey × mauve.

GREYWING (*Dilute*)

The recessive factor producing greywing dilutes the dark pigmentation (menalin) in the wings and striations to approximately 50 percent of the normal intensity. The body color is diluted proportionally. Greywings can be bred in all colors and varieties except the pastels which are recessive to greywing. In general, greywings seem to fail in head, size and spots. Breeding to good normals will help to upgrade the stock but, since greywing is recessive to normal, only normals/greywing will be bred in the first generation. Greywing × greywing will produce all greywing stock, unless the greywings in the breeding team carry the white (pastel) recessive in which case 50 percent of the greywing poults will be split to pastel, if one parent is split to white. If both parents are split to white, the results will be 50 percent greywing/white, 25 percent greywing and 25 percent white or pure pastel. Only test matings can segregate the pure from the split birds.

WHITE (*Pastel*)

Since it is a pure recessive (homozygous), the best breeding to produce white is by breeding white to white. As in the case of any recessive color, if improvement is needed, a normal, strong in the wanted virtues, should be introduced. The resulting chicks will be normal/white and by breeding brother to sister or mating a normal/white back to the pure white, some pure recessive progeny will result.

White can be bred in sky, cobalt or mauve, since it is the pastel phase in the blue series. Suffusion varies from very light, almost pure white, to a deeper suffusion which closely approaches the color depth of the clearwing. Cinnamons can be introduced into the stud of whites of light suffusion, since the cinnamon tends to further reduce color intensity.

This is a nice young hen. Note the excellent depth of bib.

With the appearance of the albino and the clearwing blue, the white has lost favor as an exhibition bird.

CLEARWING (*whitewing—yellow-wing*)*

This mutation is recessive to normal but dominant to pastel

(white, yellow). The depth and brilliance of the body color, which is about 90 percent that of the normal varieties, and the whiteness or bright yellow of the wings brings a rich vividness to this variety, though body color depth and wing markings vary greatly. It seems the lighter the wings the less brilliant the body color. The aim of the clearwing breeder, of course, is depth of body color combined with purity in wings.

This will be difficult to achieve. To bring the needed exhibition virtues into the clearwing stock it is necessary to breed in good normals. When these wanted exhibition traits have been firmly fixed in the variety so that clearwing can be bred to clearwing and produce exhibition stock, then selection can take place for clearness of wings and deep and vivid body color. The clearwing can be bred in all the basic color shades.

Clearwing × white or yellow (pastel) will produce all clearwing/pastel unless the clearwing parent is split pastel. Then only 50 percent of the young will be clearwing/pastel, the remainder, pastel. Though this breeding can give you an immediate stock of clearwings in either the green or blue series, it is not recommended. Normal × clearwing will eventually bring you much better birds. A clearwing–opaline combined produces the lovely opaline self.

FULL-BODIED GREYWINGS

When the clearwing is crossed with the greywing varieties, a strange genetic linkage occurs. The two varieties combine to produce a greywing with full body color approximately 90 percent of the normal body color and possessing the rich sheen of the clearwing. Both varieties can be produced in the same nest as can normal greywings. The full-bodied greywing is beautiful in the cobalt shade. Production of this lovely color variety is more fully explained in Chapter 10.

YELLOW FACE

This mutation in the blue series is a dominant of varied penetrance. Though it can be carried by green-series birds, the normal yellow mask of this color hides it. The yellow face can possess

---

* Dilute (greywing), pastel (white), and clearwing are varied manifestations of the same gene (*alleles*). Therefore a normal color intensity bird cannot be split to more than one of these varieties.

single or double factors of the penetration modifiers. A single-factor bird will show partial dominance and, when bred to normal white face, produces approximately 50 percent yellow face. The double-factor yellow face will produce 100 percent yellow face.

Color intensity modifiers, which can be labelled Type 1, 2, and 3, dictate the manifestation and control of spread in this mutation. Type 1 limits the tinted areas to mask and tail. Type 2 (deeper in intensity), allows the yellow to spread to the wings and upper breast. Type 3 permits a yellow wash to completely cover the bird so that many Type 3 birds cannot easily be distinguished from greens. Type 1 is the limited tinting desired in the exhibition bird. Types 2 and 3 give us the so-called "seafoams," "sea greens," "luminous" (in the pastel), and "butter creams" in the albino. Double-factor yellow faces, when bred together, can produce all white face young which, in turn, when bred to normal white face will produce yellow face young.*

RAINBOWS

The lovely rainbow is not a new mutation. It is a combination of three other mutations in the blue series—yellow face, Type 2, opaline (sex linked) and clearwing. By the proper mating of opaline self (clearwing) × full body colored opaline greywings, with one of the partners carrying the yellow face factor, one can produce, in the same nest, rainbows, yellow face full-bodied greywings and selfs. (*See* Chapter 10).

DOMINANT PIED (*clearflight*)

As the name implies this variety can genetically exhibit partial or complete dominance when bred to any other variety. The autosomal (non-sex-linked) gene which controls the manifestation of dominant pied inheritance can be present in either single or

---

*Apparently there are several forms of yellow faces, including the golden face. Some of these forms have similar behavior patterns and can combine, others cannot. Instead of being a genetic additive in the blue series, it could be a restrictive factor which originated in the green series, restricting the yellow on the body of green birds to the head, wings, and tail feathers. This would explain how a two-factor yellow face can be white faced and able to produce yellow face chicks; it possesses a double dose of the yellow restricting factor and is therefore white faced. If you are selecting for eventually the least yellow body wash, select chicks which exhibit the least amount of yellow in the short tail feathers.

double dose one or two factors. The single-factor pied bred to normal will produce 50 percent pied young. Double-factor pied mated to normal produces all pied young.

Dominant pieds of obvious heredity can be recognized in the nest before the baby down covers the skull by the small, pink island of skin on the back of the skull, surrounded by normal black pigmented skin. When the down grows in, the pink area produces light feathering that forms the pied nape spot. Similar pinkness on the wings forccast eventual light flight feathers. Cocks display more light feathers than hens, a male secondary sexual plumage ratio thought to be controlled by various hormones under genetic control.

The most obvious pied indication is the square and sometimes irregular spot of white on the back of the head. Sometimes this is accompanied by white flight feathers and can spread from these limited areas to the bleaching of more than three quarters of the feathering to present a grizzled appearance called "frosted."

The less obvious characteristic of the dominant pied is a lessening of color intensity throughout, a softening of pigmentation quite noticeable in the young. Another characteristic in this variety is the tint of body color spangling the wings, similar to that of the opaline. This is particularly noticeable in the cocks. Frequently, a bird which is genetically a pied, and thus capable of producing pieds, does not show the typical white nape spot, white flights or other obvious indications of its pied heritage and is disposed of by its owner as a non-pied because the color dilution so typical of this variety is not recognized. When mature, the dominant pied exhibits a plumage sheen similar to the clearwing.

Since it is dominant, improvement in type can be accomplished by mating pied to excellent normal. Select for the nape spot and whiteness of the ten flight feathers in the wings. Such selection will not be easy since the pied white expresses itself in various degrees and areas. In this respect it is like the grizzle factor in pigeons and in all probability has a similar and complicated genetic formula which will not permit easy confinement to specific areas of distribution (variable penetrance).

DANISH PIED (recessive)

The Danish pied has had many aliases of which "harlequin" is

The ideal Recessive Pied on the left, and the ideal Clear-Flighted Pied on the right as approved and adopted by the Pied Budgerigar Society of England, from the painting by R. A. Vowles.

perhaps the best known. Genetically they are an entirely different mutation than the dominant pied. This Danish variety is recessive and the plumage is particularly vivid where the color shows against the large bleached areas which are yellow in the green series and white in the blue series.

Generally, much greater areas show the typical albinistic patches than in the dominant pied. Vertical division of the breast, with the top section white or yellow and the bottom area in bright color is typical in the Danish. Often sexing in the young is difficult because of lack of color in the cere.

The "harlequin" mutation took the fancy by storm but, on the whole, has never been bred up to exhibition standard. The variety seems to possess a factor for smallness in head and size. The only way the breeder can hope to overcome this failing is by breeding Danish pied to excellent normal which throws normal/pied. Brother and sister matings of the progeny from this breeding will produce 25 percent visible pieds. Consistent crossing back to quality normals is the only solution to the production of exhibition-type Danish pieds.

BLACK-EYED CLEARS

This variety displays the result of pigmentation lack when pushed to the ultimate by the crossing of the two pied strains, the dominant pied and the recessive, or Danish pied—this breeding can result in a clear yellow color unmarked, in the green series, and a pure white in the blue series, similar to the lutino and albino, but with the very important exception that the name, *Black-Eyed Clear*, indicates. Dominant pied × Danish pied will produce dominant pied (clearflight) split to Danish pied. When the resulting split young are bred back to Danish a portion of the chicks will be clears, and clear × clear will produce more clears.

Do not breed lutino or albino into this variety to develop type, for these two varieties are sex-linked with entirely different breeding behavior. Luckily one of the two varieties necessary to produce clears is the dominant pied which can be constantly improved in type by breeding to normals and yet throw a percentage of pieds. This improvement, through the dominant pied, can be utilized to effect advancement in type in the clear.

FALLOW

There are several genetic mutations in the fallow variety. The best known are the English and the German fallow. In crossing some of these varieties, though basically fallows, the result is normal chicks. It is therefore necessary for the breeder to be certain that his fallow breeding partners are of the same genetic family. Unlike the other red-eyed varieties, lutino and albino which exhibit sex-linked inheritance, the fallow is a recessive.

It is not, as a variety, comparable to older varieties in type and size; therefore, breeding to large quality normals can aid in establishing better exhibition characteristics in the fallow. Since the fallow is recessive, the mating normal × fallow will produce all normals/fallow and no true fallows can be produced until the second generation. The fallow is a pleasantly soft-hued, sweet tempered bird that can be bred in any color.*

Sex-Linked Varieties

The mode of inheritance in the sex-linked varieties is clarified in Chapter 10. The varieties represented in this group of handsome budgerigars are the opaline, cinnamon, lutino and albino—the latter two, variations of the pigmentation loss that accompanies albinism and displaying the typical red eye of such specimens. Sex-linked varieties are easy to establish in any stud by the very nature of their genetic relationship.

OPALINE

The opaline mutation brings us a change in pattern accompanied by a slight reduction in basic body color. New mutations generally take a great deal of upgrading before reaching exhibition quality. But the opaline achieved the wanted improvements in a comparatively short time, seeming to lend itself easily to improvement. Thus, in many instances, the exhibition opaline can be used to improve normal strains. Particularly is this so in depth of bib and size of necklace spots and, to a lesser degree, in head. It is not uncommon for the breeder of normals to use opalines to produce splits in order to improve spot size in his stock.

Opaline mated with opaline is a good breeding and will produce all opalines. Opaline paired with any other color or variety will, if the opaline used is a quality bird, bring good results.

The most difficult achievement in opaline breeding is to produce birds with as clear a mantle as possible and a clear "V" (the area on the back between the wings) and, at the same time, to hold the full markings on the wings. It is better to hold the wing markings (as in the normal) and show slight striations in the "V" than to produce the clear "V" and erase markings from the wings.

In the opaline the white feathering on the wings and part of the white mantle is tinted by the body color.

---

*There is also in existence, an American fallow, distinct from the other varieties mentioned. This variation possesses a greater depth of color which closely approaches normal intensity. It is either a fallow mutation in its own right, or one of the older varieties which has progressed to a mutational extreme. The fallow phenotype is, genetically, the result of a recessive autosomal mutation.

well marked Opaline Australian Pied. This bird, of definite exhibition quality, shows the desired large necklace spots and nice, deep bib wanted in this variety as well as the normal colors. Bred, exhibited, and photographed in Germany.

CINNAMON

Here is a beautiful variety which has made tremendous strides forward in the last few years, toward higher and higher exhibition quality. At the moment some of the finest budgerigars in this country are cinnamon or of cinnamon breeding, as a result of cinnamon imports from England. Such stock can bring improvement to any stud.

Cinnamons exhibit the effect in their body color of the dilution factor which turns the normal black striations on back, head and wings to cinnamon brown. The result is a softening in body color and, in the blue series, a beautiful soft contrast of warm and cold coloration. The fineness of feather texture in this variety lends a smoothness to the outline only paralleled by the Australian grey. Cocks exhibit greater richness in shade and markings than do hens.

In the nest, cinnamon chicks display a reddish cinnamon through the closed eyelid before the eyes have opened. The feet are quite pink and the down of youngsters, white or yellow.

Breed cinnamon × cinnamon, or cinnamon to any other color or variety if the cinnamon used is of the fine exhibition type seen in so many shows lately. Normals split to cinnamon will frequently exhibit the fine feather texture which is the cinnamon's heritage.

LUTINO (Redeye)

The Lutino has been bred up to fine show quality in the past few years. Many of these albinistic specimens in the green series have taken first, second, third or fourth best in shows.

This color type can also be found in a non-sex-linked variety, but this type of lutino is almost extinct so we will concern ourselves only with the sex-linked variety. This is true also of the albino discussed below.

With the quality apparent in the good lutinos of today, lutino bred with lutino is the best mating. Should improvements be needed in your lutino strain, the best outcross would be to an exhibition type light yellow green or Australian grey green.

ALBINO (Redeye)

As the lutino masks normal color in the green series so the albino masks normal color in the blue series. Pure white is wanted without evidence of a blue sheen on the body. The albino has not reached the improvement so obvious in the lutino. To progress in type and size, outcrossing is generally necessary. The best matings to produce better albinos are, lutino × albino, or cinnamon or Australian grey cinnamon × albino.

The newest mutation to attain popularity is the Australian Banded Pied. Like the Dutch Pied this mutation is dominant. It exhibits the typical head patch of the pied. The wings are not just white flighted (or yellow flighted in the green variety), but should show a solidity of white or yellow over the whole wing area. Tail feathers should be white and there should be a band of white horizontally dividing the basic breast color. Legs and feet are pink. Spots should be as evident as in the normal Budgie, but often the pied bleaching extends into the mask partially or fully masking the spots and cheek flashes. The basic color of the Australian Pied is rich and carries an added irridescence. The area (color and pied) proportions are difficult to hold, particularly on the breast. In the author's experience with this variety it would appear that many color modifiers have been established as part of the geneology of the Australian Pied and carried as recessives. But, being a dominant variety, it has been comparatively easy to develop the variety to a high standard of perfection by the introduction of top normals and opalines so that today the Australian Dominant Pied, in the best specimens, is almost equal in conformation to the finest normals.

The reader should, by now, know superficially how best to employ his basic stock for superior production but—only superficially. To achieve the best results from any livestock breeding one must know the principles of basic genetics and the breeding procedures which are the outgrowth of that knowledge. The next two chapters deal with these subjects and are the two most important chapters in this book. This information is placed before other informative chapters because the knowledge it imparts will not only aid you in achieving the most from your breeding results but will also enable you to select more knowingly that initial stock which will form the basis of your stud.

Genetics, the study of inheritance, and the ability to best make use of the various known breeding procedures, is the key to all breeding success. Most layman breeders retreat from the word "genetics" as something which is beyond the scope of their understanding. Few, if any, budgerigar breeders are scientists, geneticists or higher mathematicians, and they need not be. For in the two following chapters will be found all you need to know about this fascinating subject, written so that the lay reader can understand and, what is more important, make use of the basic precepts.

Chapter 2
MODES OF INHERITANCE

Of all the creatures known to man that fly or walk or crawl the earth, few display such frequency of obvious genetic mutation as the budgerigar. It is these mutations within the gene structure that give us the many beautiful variations from which to choose. Most of the genetic studies done with budgerigars have been concentrated in this interesting field of genetic color change, but, in this chapter and the one to follow, divorce from your mind all thoughts of color and apply that which you read to the various elements that compose type, balance and structure in the budgerigar.

Let us first clear away the debris of old untruths and superstition in regard to inheritance so that we may, more clearly, evaluate the truth. The inheritance of acquired characteristics due to the influence of environment, and the theory of birthmarking are both fallacious and must be discarded in the light of present-day knowledge. The theories of telegony, that the sire of one clutch can influence future nests by the same hen when bred to a different cock, and the supposition that a hen, bred many times to the same cock, will become so "saturated" with his "blood" that she will produce progeny always of his type, even when mated to an entirely different male, are both old wives tales.

By far the most widely believed of all the many false theories of inheritance has been the "blood" theory which postulates that the blood is the vehicle through which all inheritable material is passed from one generation to the next. The phraseology we employ in our breeding terms such as "blood-lines," "pure-blooded," "percentage of blood," attest to the strength of this theory.

What must be clearly and decisively understood is that the genes which determine inheritable characteristics are isolated in the body from any and all environmental influences. What the budgerigar host does or has done to him influences them, the genes, not at all.

MENDELIAN EXPECTATION CHART

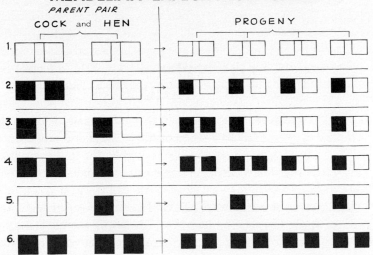

The six possible ways in which a pair of determiners can unite. Ratios are exact only in matings 1, 2 and 6 when applied to a limited number of nests.

The true facts of heredity were found in spite of persistent false theories and superstition, and in the history of science there is no more dramatic story. This truth was not arrived at in some fine, endowed scientific laboratory agleam with the mysterious implements of research. The scene was instead a small garden in Moravia, now a part of Czechoslovakia. There Gregor Johann Mendel, a Moravian monk, planted and crossed several varieties of common peas and quietly recorded the differences that occurred through many generations. Over a period of eight years this remarkable man continued his research. In 1865 he brought his findings before the local naturalist and historian society and his scholarly paper was printed in their bulletin.

Few people read the bulletin and those who did were unimpressed. Amazingly enough, Mendel's theory of inheritance, the basis of all the modern advances in genetic research, was cast aside and forgotten for thirty-four years. It seemed that the most important scientific discovery of the nineteenth century was destined to be lost to mankind. Then, sixteen years after Mendel's death, in 1900, the dusty old bulletin was found, the theory printed in its yellowed pages evaluated and Mendel's great work was given to the world.

In his experiments Mendel found and identified the units of heredity. He discovered that when two individual plants which differed in a specific or unit trait were mated, one trait appeared in the progeny and one did not. The trait that was visible he called the *dominant* trait, and the one which was not visible he named the *recessive* trait. He proposed that all traits, such as type, size and color, are transmitted by means of units in the sex cells and that these units are individually pure for a certain trait—let us say, green or blue—but can never be a mixture of both green and blue. Therefore, from a green parent which is pure for that trait, only green units are transmitted, and from a blue parent only blue units can be passed on. But when one parent is green and one is blue, a hybrid occurs which transmits both the green and blue units in specific amounts. The hybrid itself will exhibit the color of the dominant parent unit, yet carry the other color as a recessive (in budgerigars the green/blue). This theory applies to all the other varied characteristics of form, type, size and mentality, as well as to color. Various combinations of units were tried by Mendel, and he found that there were six possible ways in which a pair of determiners or genes (Mendel's "units") could be combined with a similar pair of units. The simple Mendelian law of ratio holds true in the actual breeding of all living things, whether plants, fish, mice, humans or budgerigars.

From the union of a male sperm and a female egg cell during the process of copulation, new life makes its beginning. Each of the male sperm cells has a nucleus which contains one set of chromosomes, small packages of "units" or *genes* which are the inheritable material. The female egg contains a like set of chromosomes. The new life formed by the union of sperm cell and egg cell then possesses two sets of chromosomes, one from the sire and one from the dam. Two things happen when the sperm cell enters the egg, it starts the egg developing and it adds a set of chromosomes to the set already in the egg. *Here is the secret of heredity.* For in the chromosomes lie the living genes that form the genetic pattern of the unborn young. Thus we see that all eventual characteristics are transmitted to our budgie from its sire and dam through tiny living cells called genes, the connecting links between the chick and its ancestors.

The chromosomes, actually "packages" of genes, resemble long, paired strings of beads. Each pair is alike, yet differing from the like partners of the next pair. In the female budgerigar we find the exception to this rule, for in the hen, there is one pair of chromosomes that are not alike. These are the sex chromosomes, and in the hen they are different from those in the cock bird for the male possesses a like pair while the female does not.

If we designate the male chromosome as X, then the male chromosome pair is XX. The female carries an X chromosome, but also a Y chromosome. If the male X chromosome unites with the female X chromosome, the resulting chick will be an XX individual, a cock. Should the male X chromosome unite with the female Y chromosome in the egg, then the poult that emerges from the egg will be an XY, a hen. It is, therefore, a matter of chance as to what sex the offspring of any given mating will be, since sperm is capricious and fertilization is random.

The genes which dictate sex-linked inheritance in budgerigars are located on this X (sex) chromosome, hence the term "sex-linked." A cock in the sex-linked series can carry the sex-linked gene on one or both of his X chromosomes. A cock which is split for a sex-linked characteristic carries the sex-linked genes on only one of his X chromosomes. A cock who is visually of a sex-linked variety has the sex-linked genes resident on both X chromosomes. The hen must carry the sex-linked genes on her X chromosome to exhibit sex-linked traits, since a Y chromosome does not carry the sex-linked characteristic.

Thus a cock may carry, potentially as well as visually, sex-linked characteristics in the split or recessive state. A hen must visibly display the trait or not carry it at all, she cannot be split to a sex-linked character. Incidentally, this sex gene chromatic design is unique in birds, insects, and fish. In most all other living species the male of the species carries the odd pair of sex chromosomes (XY), while the female carries the matched pair (XX).

Each individual possesses these paired strings of chromosomes which dictate genetic heritage. When fertilization takes place, each partner of the mated pair lends but one of each of its own pair to the progeny, in the same manner in which only one of the sex chromosomes from each breeding partner is passed on. Selection is random so it is easy to see how brother and sister poults in the same nest may display much variation in type.

The actual embryonic growth of the chick is a process of division of cells to form more and more cells and at each cell division the two sets of chromosomes provided by the parents also divide, until all the many divisions of cells and chromosomes have reached an amount necessary to form a new, complete, living entity. Then the chick breaks from the egg in all its nudity and helplessness.

Paired chromosomes.

Photographs 3 through 8 shows in detail the pairing of chromosomes in various animals and plants. (3) is a grasshopper; (4) is the tip of a plant; (5) is a pollen grain; (6) is also a pollen grain; (7) is another root tip; (8) is still another root tip.

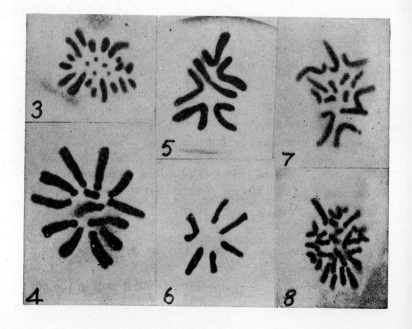

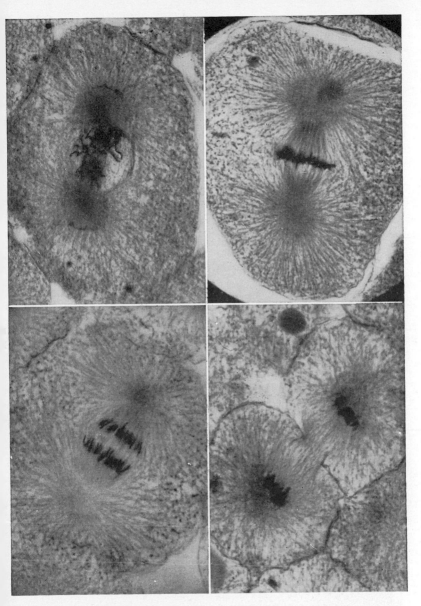

On page 48 the illustrations show in general the mitosis, or chromosome split. Here we see in detail chromosome splitting step by step. Upper left: the cell getting ready with the chromosomes a jumbled mass in the center. Upper right: the chromosomes lining up. Lower left: the chromosomes splitting into two pieces. Lower right: the two cells nearly separated from each other. These are actual photomicrographs shown through the courtesy of the General Biological Supply House, Chicago, Illinois.

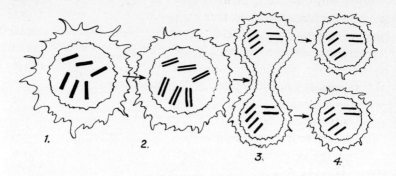

BEHAVIOR OF CHROMOSOMES IN CELL DIVISION: 1. Single cell with three pairs of chromosomes. **2.** The same cell about to divide with the chromosomes splitting sideways. **3.** Cell dividing, half of each chromosome in each new nucleus. **4.** Division completed.

Photomicrograph, greatly enlarged, showing various cells in different stages of mitosis, stage where the chromosomes split to form the nucleii of two cells. The illustration ab shows more clearly what the photomicrographs show. Courtesy of the General Biolog Supply House, Chicago, Illinois.

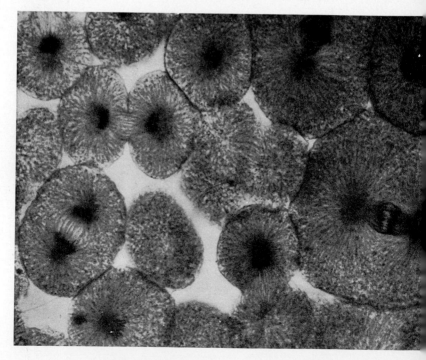

What will this chick be like? He will be what his controlling genes make him. We know that his parents have contributed one gene of each kind to their chick, and this gene (which they have separately given him) is but one of the two which each parent possesses for a particular characteristic. Since he has drawn these determiners at random, they can be either dominant or recessive genes, so scrambled that some are one some the other. His dominant traits become visible as he develops, but his recessive heritage remains largely hidden.

There are rules which allow us to recognize dominant and recessive traits that are useful in summarizing what we know of the subject at the present time. These findings are important because not only dominants can appear visually, recessives can be visual too when the individual carries all recessives, and no dominants, for a particular characteristic.

To illustrate this more clearly, let us take, as an example, a budgie which is green/blue. We know that green is dominant to blue. The bird, therefore, is visually a green but carries the recessive blue in the hidden state. When mated to a blue this green/blue bird's pairs of color genes, one for green, one for blue, will join the hen's color genes which are pure recessive blue. Those genes of the cocks which are dominant, or green, will produce green/blue offspring, but those which are blue, pairing with the hen's blue genes, will produce blue progeny which represents the visual manifestation of a pair of recessive determiners.

We can see then, how useful rules can be which show us how to differentiate between dominant and recessive manifestation.

We can be reasonably sure that a dominant trait (1) does not skip a generation; (2) will effect a relatively large number of the progeny; (3) will be carried only by effected individuals; (4) minimizes the danger of continuing undesirable characteristics in a strain or family; and makes the breeding formula of the individual more certain.

With recessive traits we note that: (1) the trait may skip one or more generations; (2) on the average a relatively small percentage of the individuals in the strain carry the trait; (3) only those individuals which carry a pair of determiners for the trait exhibit it visually; (4) individuals which carry only one determiner for the trait (splits) can be ascertained only by breeding results; (5) the trait must come through both parents.

Many breeders disagree as to which parent most influences the young, the cock or the hen. Genetically, each parent contributes equally to the shaping of their progeny, since the chicks receive 50 percent of their germ plasm from each, though one parent may possess so many matched pairs of dominant genes that the influence it exerts on its chicks will lead the breeder to believe that the chicks received most of their inheritable material from this parent. An individual carrying two sets of determiners, one from each parent, when put up to breed, passes only one set of determiners on to its offspring. It would seem then that the genetic influence of one of the offspring's grandparents would be completely lost and the chick has inherited the germ plasm from only two of its grandparents, not four. But this is not true. Selection of the genes is governed by chance, and chromosomes cross over, so it is possible for the chick's four grandparents to contribute an equal 25 percent of all the genes inherited or various and individual percentages, one grandparent contributing more, another less. It is even possible for the chick to inherit no genes at all from one grandparent and 50 percent from another.

The genes themselves are of chemical composition, are living cells and, as has been mentioned before, are securely isolated from outside influence. Environment can effect an individual but not his germ plasm. For instance, if a chick's nutritional needs are not fully provided for during the vital period of growth, his potential will not be attained; but regardless of outward appearance, his germ plasm remains inviolate and capable of passing on to the next generation the potential that was denied the chick by improper feeding.

Breeding winning exhibition budgerigars would be a fairly simple procedure if all characteristics were governed by simple mendelian factors, but this is not so. Single genes are not solely responsible for single characteristics. The complexity of any section of the body and its dependence upon other parts in order to function properly makes it obvious that we must deal generally with interlocking blocks of controlling genes. This becomes too complicated for the average breeder but, knowing what he now does about the behavior of genetic characteristics, the breeder can simplify and make good use of the knowledge he has acquired. He can take any section of the budgerigar's anatomy and ascertain through the rules for dominant and recessive traits, whether this trait is dominant or recessive. He can then refer to the mendelian expectation chart and find how best to improve or eliminate the trait.

n the left is a dominant Australian Pied, of nice type, cellent spots, and well marked. On the right is an example the recessive Pied (Harlequin). This is a very nice n of this variety.

To illustrate, let us pick such a trait, a protruding beak, which the breeder wishes to eliminate from his stock. We will assume he has a fine cock, marred by this trait. It crops up occasionally in his strain and he has "selected against it." He knows by consulting the rules mentioned that this is a recessive trait and, to be visible in this cock, the bird must carry a pair of determiners for it, so it is a *pure* recessive.

He then checks the mendelian chart and, using the open, white squares for recessive symbols, he sees that he must breed this cock to a hen whose dominant pair of determiners, for correction of this trait, are symbolized by the filled in, black squares. He makes his breeding. If all the chicks are free of the protruding mandible trait he knows that the mother hen was dominant for the proper beak placement and he knows also that each chick carries a recessive for the protruding beak. If he finds a ratio of approximately 50 percent of the progeny from this breeding still possess protruding beaks, he knows that the hen also carries this fault in the hidden, recessive state. From either of these breedings he will of course select the chicks which are visibly good but, as he now knows, carry the harmful recessive. He can breed these chicks together with the results shown on the chart, or he can use the better mating, if he has a breeding partner purely dominant for the wanted trait. By breeding he can determine which of the chicks are purely dominant for this wanted trait. This will eliminate the protruding beak character forever from this strain, unless he eventually brings in an outcross that again carries the trait for protruding beak in the recessive or split form.

Since they are living cells, genes can and do change, or mutate. In budgerigars we are well aware of this. It is thought now that many more gene mutations occur in the individual than were formerly suspected. The great majority are not dramatic, easily seen mutations, such as the color mutation or the long flight mutation in budgies, but are so small in general scope that they are overlooked. Other mutations occur within the bird where they cannot be seen and therefore go unnoticed. The mutations easily recognized are the ones we select for or against according to our tastes or whether they direct us toward or away from our goal. Again, with the vagary inherent in all living things, the mutated gene can change back again to its original form.

Remember that it is *not* the bird, but the genes that are dominant or recessive. We now know that a budgie can contain in each of his body cells a dominant and a recessive gene. When this occurs the bird is said to be *heterozygous*. The opposite to the *heterozygous* individual is a bird who carries two genes of the same kind in its cells, either two dominants or two recessives, and this bird is said to be *homozygous*. A bird can be heterozygous for one or more traits, and homozygous for other traits. The loss of a gene, the gain of a gene or the process of change among genes, is known as *mutation*, and the bird affected is called a *mutant*.

Every budgerigar in the world, cock or hen, is not just one budgerigar, but two. Every living thing is a Jekyll and Hyde, shadow and substance. The budgerigar that we see is the phenotype, the physical manifestation of the interaction of genotypic characters and environment. The bird we do not see, the genotype, is the gene-complex, or total collection of the genes. Though we cannot see this "shadow" bird it is as much a part of the budgerigar as the bird we see. The visual bird is easily evaluated, but the invisible bird, the genotype, must also be as clearly familiar to the breeder as the visual bird, for both "shadow and substance" equally contribute to the generations to come. Without understanding the complete genetic picture of any particular bird, we cannot hope to successfully use that bird to accomplish specific results. In order to understand and evaluate, we must delve into the bird's ancestry and assess the genetic background until the shadow becomes as clearly discernible as the substance and we can evaluate the bird's genetic worth as a whole; for this bird is but the containing vessel, the custodian of a specific pattern of heredity.

Since obvious mutation in the budgerigar has been so frequent, the necessity for the breeder's understanding of the fundamental modes of inheritance and the breeding techniques employed becomes imperative. For in a species which displays so many mutational effects, variation is also progressive and accompanies mutation. It is, therefore, more difficult to breed toward a set standard of perfection. But, if basic genetic knowledge is employed, mutation and variation become the breeder's tools.

In effect and influence mutations do not vary too greatly in individual species. It is interesting to note that genetic studies of the fruit fly indicate that about one quarter of all genetic mutations are lethal or semi-lethal. Sterility is produced in one or both of the sexes in approximately 15 to 20 percent of all fruit fly mutations. And there is a varied reduction in vitality and vigor in almost all new mutations. These mutations occurred spontaneously from natural causes. It is necessary to make this last statement because, though mention has been made that genes cannot be affected by outside influences such as environment, and this still holds true, there are exceptions. X-rays, drugs, and certain kinds of radiation, essentially nuclear radiation, can effect genetic changes in inheritable tissue. Such changes are, of course, neither spontaneous nor natural.*

The study of genetics continues as men of science delve ever deeper into cause and effect in this study of life forces. What we know today of inheritance is of immeasurable importance in the advancement of animal breeding, removing much of the guesswork from our operations. Yet we do not know enough, and any life-form is so complicated and unstable, that it cannot be reduced to the realm of purity with a definite answer to every problem. Life, spontaneous and varying as it must be, leads us to believe that even with the greater knowledge the future will undoubtedly bring, the breeding of better budgerigars will remain a combination of science, art and instinct, to ever lend fascination and inner reward to our hobby.

---

* Great advances in genetics were achieved when the science was approached from the chemical angle. In 1940, a new and genuinely pliable genetic material was found in *Neurospora crassa*, a mold. The nutritional elements necessary for the mold to thrive upon were established. Thereafter spores of the mold were subjected to X-rays causing various artificially induced mutations. These mutations did not generally thrive on the nutritional elements utilized by the basic natural mold. Some required specific vitamins, amino acids or other growth producing chemicals, which the natural mold produced within itself from the basic diet. It was also found that, when mated to natural mold, the mutant molds transmitted this need for extra dietary essentials to its progeny in the accepted Mendelian ratio. This information can be adjusted to fit the pattern of mysterious ills that accompany so great a mutational departure from the norm as the long flight.

The basic governing entity, determining heredity and governing all cells and all life, is a large molecule labelled DNA, found in the chromosomes. The symbol DNA (deoxyribonucleic acid) bulks large in present-day genetic research, for it is believed that DNA is the guiding force behind growth and reproduction. DNA, like a chemical Svengali, uses cells for its Trilby, giving commands which the cells are powerless to resist. Geneticists now believe that DNA exists in all living things, including virus and bacteria, and that all living things, including man, are but vehicles for DNA's constant reproduction of more DNA.

Chapter 3
BASIC BREEDING TECHNIQUES

In this modern world of rapid pace, specialization and easy, varied entertainment, artistic activity and creativeness has been all but lost to the ordinary individual. Self expression is a natural need of man, and we who breed budgerigars are extremely fortunate, for in the process we can give full rein to that inherent and necessary creativeness, to express our needs, our personalities, in living flesh and beauty. We have the power to create an animate work of art if we skillfully use the proven tools that are ready to our hand.

These tools are the basic breeding techniques that have been used with success in all forms of livestock breeding. Now that we have absorbed some of the basic facts of heredity, we can, with greater understanding, examine the various kinds of breeding which can be used to perpetuate wanted characteristics. We have learned that within the design of the germ plasm variation occurs. But, within the breed itself as a whole, we have an average, or norm, which the majority of budgerigars mirror. The same is true of any individual number of birds in any specific aviary. To simplify let us consider the birds in your aviary as your "aviary population." This population consists of budgies which we can broadly label, good, average and below average. Now, draw a straight horizontal line on a piece of paper and label this line the "norm." Above this line draw another and label it, "above norm." This line represents your top birds and the length of this line will be much shorter than that of the "norm" line. Below the "norm" line draw still another line, designating this "below norm." This represents the birds in your population which possess faults you do not wish to perpetuate. Your breeding objective is to shorten, with each season's breeding, the "below norm" and lengthen the "above norm" line. This is the initial step. Once you have accomplished this, within reason, your next objective is to raise your "below norm" birds up to your present "norm" line, your "norm" line to your "above norm" indication and so establish your top group of budgies beyond anything you have yet bred. As time and breeding seasons progress, your stock should improve to such an extent that the birds which were "above norm" last season would, this season, be in the group labelled "norm." Select for each season's breeding only those birds which are in the "above norm" grouping and a few of the very best, in visual type and breeding background from the "norm" group.

A Best-in-Show Normal Sky Cock exhibiting the characteristics which made him a champion.

If we are to achieve the greatest good from any breeding program, there are four important traits our breeding pairs must possess and which, throughout our breeding population, must never depart drastically from normal.

The first is *fertility*. The lack of this essential in any degree must be guarded against diligently.

The second is *vigor*. Loss of vigor, or hardiness, and its allied ills, such as lowered resistance to disease, lack of appetite, etc., will lead to disaster.

Longevity of production is the third important trait. An individual bird of great worth who represents a fortunate combination of excellent genetic characteristics which he dominantly passes to his offspring must be useful for a long time after his (or her) worth is recognized by the progeny produced.

No vices is the fourth important trait. A hen or cock that savages its young, is a feather-picker, breaks eggs before hatching, etc., will in all probability pass these tendencies on to its progeny since mental characteristics are inherited as well as type and color; certain breeding techniques could heighten these vices to the extreme in your strain.

The "norm" can be likened to the force of gravity, possessing a powerful pull toward itself, so that regression toward the average is strong, even though only "above norm" birds were used as breeding partners. The same holds true of birds bred from budgies "below norm," but from these you will get a lesser number which reach the population average and a greater number which remain "below norm." Occasionally a budgerigar of superior type is produced by a poor family, but inevitably this bird is useless in the breeding cage because he will produce all his objectionable family traits and few of the fortuitous virtues he himself displays.

From the breeder's view it is far better to use an average individual from above average stock than a top individual from below-average stock. It is also true that many times a fine, frequent best-in-show budgerigar, produces average progeny while his average nest-brother produces above-average young. This is not so strange when we consider the fact that the individual bird is the custodian of his germ-plasm and it is this genetic material that produces the get, not the individual. In the instance just cited, due to variation in the germ plasm, the top bird does not possess the correct genetic combinations that his average brother does and so cannot produce stock of comparative value.

The following breeding practices can be utilized for the betterment of your stock. Regardless of the technique one follows, there usually comes a time when it is necessary to incorporate one or more of the other forms into the breeding program in order to concentrate genetic factors or to introduce new ones which are imperative for over-all balance. Outcross breeding is not recommended as a consistent practice. Rather, it is a valuable adjunct to the other methods if corrective measures are needed.

INBREEDING

By breeding father to daughter, half brother to half sister, son to mother, and, the closest inbreeding of all, sister to brother, stability and purity of inherited material is obtained. Specifically, inbreeding concentrates both good features and faults, strengthens dominants and brings recessives into the open where they can be seen and evaluated. It supplies the breeder with the only control possible over prepotency and homozygosity, or the combining and balancing of similar genetic characters. It will not produce either degeneration or faults. It merely concentrates weaknesses already present so that they can be recognized and eliminated. This applies to both physical and psychic-virtues and faults.

The most important phases of inbreeding are: to choose as nearly faultless partners as possible, both in themselves and their breeding; to cull, or select, rigidly from the resultant progeny.

Selection is always important, regardless of the breeding technique employed, but with inbreeding it becomes imperative. Most successful inbreeding programs have as their base, a bird which was either inbred or line bred. To the breeder, the inbred bird represents an individual whose breeding formula has been so simplified that it will dependably produce foreseeable results. Though it is true that occasionally lethal faults, hitherto unsuspected in the stock, might become so drastically concentrated by inbreeding that they could threaten the extinction of a line. But such is the inherent character of germ plasm that one direct outcross will bring complete normalcy to any inbred line badly weakened by its own concentrated faults.

It is essential that the breeder have complete understanding of the merits of inbreeding, for by skillful employment he can advance his stock with greater rapidity than he thought possible. We must remember that inbreeding in itself creates neither faults nor virtues, it merely strengthens and fixes those already in the germ plasm of the individual. If the basic stock used is generally excellent, possessing but few minor faults, then inbreeding will concentrate this excellence so it can be passed on to the progeny in pure form. Inbreeding gives us greater breeding worth by its unique ability to produce prepotency and unusual similarity of type. By this we know that only through inbreeding can we establish a strain that will be stamped with certain characteristics all our own. Inbreeding brings to light hidden faults (recessives) that can be "selected against," exposing, as it were, the "skeletons in the closet." We do not correct faults by inbreeding, we merely make them recognizable so they can be seen and eliminated. The end result of inbreeding, coupled with rigid selection, is complete stability of the breeding material.

The extremes produced are an interesting development, frequently found initially in inbreeding. The average progeny is equal to the average encountered in any other form of breeding, but the extremes of good or bad are greater. By rigid selection, the extremes will close up until there is slight difference between the three gradations.

BACKCROSSING

Another type of inbreeding, which is not practiced as much as it should be, is "backcrossing." With this technique we think largely in terms of the cock budgerigar, since the element of time is involved and the male bird generally has a longer breeding life than the hen. The process involves the finding of a superior cock, so magnificent in type and pedigree that we wish to perpetuate his qualities and reproduce, as closely as we can, the prototype of this individual. To found a line on him, the cock is bred to the best hen, and the best hen chick who is similar in type to her sire is bred back to him. Again the best young hen is selected to be bred back to her sire. This continues as long as the cock can reproduce, or until genetic weaknesses make their appearance (if they do) and make further breeding impractical. If the excellent cock seems to have acquired his superiority through the genetic influence of his mother, we should first breed him to his mother and then employ the technique mentioned above in subsequent breedings. In each nest the important thing to remember is that

THE SIRE: a Best-in-Show linebred cock.

THE DAM: A winning hen, sister to the cock.

THE CHICK. A 5 month old hen, destined for high show honors. Daughter of the pair above. The result of the closest inbreeding but bred by a knowledgeable breeder from quality stock.

the hen retained for the backcross should, of course, more closely mirror her sire's type and excellence than any other chick.

LINE BREEDING

This is a broader kind of inbreeding that conserves valuable genetic characteristics by lesser concentration than inbreeding and, in a general sense, gives us some control of type but a lesser control over specific characteristics. A strain can be created by this method also. It is the technique employed by many breeders, with varied success, since it is not extreme and, therefore, relatively safe.

Line-breeding entails the selection of breeding partners who have one or more common ancestors. These individuals occur repeatedly within the first few generations, so that it can be assumed that their genetic influence molds the type of succeeding generations. It is a fact that much in successful breeding can be attributed to line breeding with outstanding individual budgerigars.

The method varies greatly in intensity. Some birds may be strongly line-bred while others only remotely so. Selection is also an important factor here, for if we line-breed to procure the specific type of a fine individual, then we must select those birds for our future breeding which most closely approach that individual in type. Otherwise our reason for line-breeding is lost. The method is similar, as you can see, to inbreeding and, particularly backcrossing, but not nearly so intense or rapid in results. In some instances, intense line breeding, particularly when the bird line-bred from is prepotent, can have almost the same effect as inbreeding.

To get the most from line-breeding, to use this method to found a strain which has definite characteristics of its own, the following recommendations will prove valuable.

1. Decide what traits are essential and what faults intolerable. Vigor and fertility along with the elements of type should be included in these essentials.

2. Develop a scoring system and score selected virtues and faults in accordance with your breeding aims. Particular stress should be put upon scoring those individual traits which need improving. Use simple scoring symbols such as E + (excellent plus), E, E −,

G+ (good plus), G, G−. Add your trait score and give each bird an overall score which is the sum total of all its scored traits. Use the same symbols as above and, when you have finished, discard any birds which rate lower than G+.

3. Line-breed consistently to the G+ or better birds which show by the progeny test that they will further improve the strain.

These rules can be applied to forming a strain with any type of breeding. Inbreeding and backcrossing, can be practised if the bird used is of exceptional quality with no outstanding faults. Outcrossing can be made to bring in wanted characteristics if they are missing from the basic stock. Relationship in the initial stock need not be too close since greater variation will offer a much wider selection of desirable trait combinations.

Every bird used in a breeding program to establish a strain must be rigidly assessed for individual and breeding excellence and the general worth of its near relatives and progeny. Once the traits wanted have been massed and concentrated in individual birds, you have established the foundation of a strain.

OUTCROSSING

Outcross breeding is the mating of budgerigars with no common ancestry.

For the breeder to exercise any control over the breeding result of an outcross mating, one of the partners should be inbred or closely line-bred. The other partner should show (in itself and by the progeny test) its dominance in the needed compensations, which are the reasons for the outcross. Outcross breeding, therefore, brings new and needed characteristics into a strain, along with generally greater vigor and usually a lack of uniformity in the young. Greater uniformity can be achieved if the birds used are of similar type. It is possible to produce excellent budgerigars by this method since it tends to conceal recessive characteristics and promote individual, visual merit. But generally this leads to lower breeding worth in the outbred bird by dispersing favorable genetic combinations and uniformity.

Outcross breeding can be likened to a jigsaw puzzle. The puzzle, where complete, is comparable to our line-bred or inbred strain. But there are a few pieces which we would like to change, and in so doing improve the finished puzzle pattern. We remove some of the pieces and replace them with other pieces differently shaped (outcrossing), but we must remember that these new pieces will effect the pieces of the original puzzle that surround them and so those surrounding pieces must then be slightly altered to fit. When this has been accomplished, the finished pattern has been altered for the better, we hope.

Outcrossing is thus used to compensate for failings. But when we speak of corrective or compensation breeding, it does not mean the breeding together of extremes to achieve an intermediate effect. We should not breed a bird of excessive backskull to a "pinhead" (no backskull at all), hoping that, by such a breeding, to get a progeny possessing normal backskulls. The result either would be excessive backskulls or no backskulls. Corrective or compensation breeding means the mating of one partner, which lacks or is faulty in any specific trait to another, visually and genetically, normal or excellent in the particular trait.

HETEROSIS

Heterosis is a comparatively new field in genetic research. The results obtained by this method of breeding in other fields (agricultural, and with swine and chickens) have been phenomenal. Extensive research is still continuing and, since genetic material can vary in its reaction and result to any given and unexplored breeding method, the inclusion of this technique, untried as yet with budgerigars does not rightly belong in this book. But it will, in all probability, arouse as much interest in the reader as it has in the author.

Briefly and simply the basis of heterosis is the breeding together of selected brothers and sisters, and this is continued for many generations to establish strains which are completely homozygous (all gene pairs alike). It seems doubtful, to the writer, that absolute homozygosity can be attained, regardless of the number of generations of complete inbreeding, due to genetic variation and small mutational effects. Yet it is necessary in this breeding method to inbreed for enough generations to arrive at the most complete homozygous result attainable. After three or four generations have been bred, test-cross matings are tried by crossing the several lines to establish which of the strain crossings will give the greatest improvements in type, size, or thriftiness. The most usable strains are then maintained. The inbreeding within the original lines is continued.

We can suppose that by the fifth generation the inbred lines will display considerable change for the worse. The birds will be smaller, less thrifty and typy, but after selection the best can be used to carry on. By the sixth or seventh generation there should be some improvement in the inbred lines, almost as though detrimental effects have been squeezed out of the lines by this intense inbreeding.

In the eighth generation the lines are crossed, a hen from one line being bred to a cock from another line. The results of this breeding can then be crossed to a partner of like breeding from different lines. If the results obtained are parallel to the results found in other fields where this method has been employed, we should get completely heterozygous young (all gene pairs opposite or unalike). The name of this method of breeding, in itself, heterosis, is borrowed from the result, heterozygosity.

These budgerigars, the result of heterosis, should be much larger, typier, more vigorous, fertile and generally more thrifty, than the original pairs with which the experiment was begun. In short, a race of what we might term *super budgerigars*. From studies in this field, the author proposes that heterosis is accom-

On the left is a typical, exaggerated Longflight, photo taken in an English aviary. On the right, a B.I.S. winning longflight green cock of some years ago that founded a show winning strain for Mr. Bennett Wood.

panied by intermediate gene frequency equilibrium, or, an essential balance of chromatic design.

To briefly sum up the information in this chapter, we find that *inbreeding* brings us fixity or stability of type and simplifies the breeding formula. It strengthens desirable dominants and brings hidden, undesirable recessives to the surface where they can be recognized and possibly corrected, sometimes by *outcrossing*, which brings desired corrections or compensation where it is necessary. *Line-breeding* is less intense than direct inbreeding, but gives us some control over strain characteristics and can be used successfully to establish a strain after definite improvement in type, by rigid selection, has been attained. *Backcrossing*, is inbreeding upon a specific individual. These breeding techniques can be employed individually, or knowingly combined to breed better budgerigars.

THE LONG FLIGHT

Before this chapter is brought to a close mention must be made of a new mutation which has aroused considerable controversy in the ranks of the fancy. This variety, the *long flight*, was not mentioned in the first chapter because it is not a color variety. It is a mutation in structural form which first made its appearance in England during the late 30's. Many breeders condemn the long flight and claim it will bring myriad ills in its wake if fused with the carefully bred strains already in existence. In fact, a furor has been aroused, both here and abroad to disqualify the long flight from exhibition competition. A few breeders hold forth for the new mutation, but their voices are weak in the thunder of mass condemnation.

This mutant has a larger skeletal structure, larger head, deeper bib and larger spots, sometimes flat-topped. The feathers that clothe the bird are wider and longer than normal to conform to the greater over-all size. Flight feathers are particularly long and coarse, the web of the primaries being much wider than normal. The wings themselves have a seemingly different placement but this, I think, is due to the greater length from wing top to the top of the head which lends the appearance of lower wing attachment. The tail feathers are long and coarse, and the bird, when sitting on the perch, frequently fans out the shorter tail feathers. Many specimens lie across the perch, and are erratic in flight.

Many claim this erratic flight is caused by a form of myopia. Others affirm that the long flight has a tendency toward idiocy. These theories are based upon observation of the eccentric flight and behavior of the bird.

The author has had no opportunity for experimental breeding with this mutation, so his knowledge of its breeding behavior is merely the result of sifting for truth amongst the opinions and experience of other breeders. From this second-hand data it would appear that the long flight is a dominant of variable penetrance and can probably possess one or two factors which would give it either partial dominance or complete dominance. The erratic flight and behavior this mutant frequently displays may, more rationally, be attributed to a lack of physical balance, due to its marked departure in structure from the typical as represented by the normally balanced budgerigar.

It is the author's considered opinion that the long flight should not be high-handedly condemned. We have been breeding toward larger size, bigger heads, deeper masks and larger throat spots and all these virtues the long flight can give us. There is a natural outer limit beyond which any trait cannot be pushed. This law of limitation within a species allows us only a limited area in which to work and seek improvements. Only by fortuitous mutation can a species go beyond this limitation and give us wider scope for improvement. We have found that fortuitous mutation in the long flight. In England this mutant is condemned and barred from competition, yet, paradoxically, many of the top, winning English budgerigars exhibit long flight characteristics, from controlled long flight inheritance.

We must not lump all long flights together, but must recognize the fact that there are good, bad, and indifferent long flights just as there are good, bad and indifferent normal birds. We cannot expect desired results unless we use a good long flight in our matings. The long flight characteristic seems to vary, so that you will find chicks in the same nest exhibiting degrees of long flightedness, from the extreme to almost normal indicating variable penetrance of the trait.

The author would like to see classes for long flights added to shows. The bird is, after all, a budgerigar, and should have individual classification as have all other mutations. This would

good longflight which closely approaches normalcy. Birds showing this degree longflightedness are frequently successfully exhibited. (Note: There are varying grees of longflightedness (variable penetrance) from the extreme to the almost normal and they can appear in the same nest.)

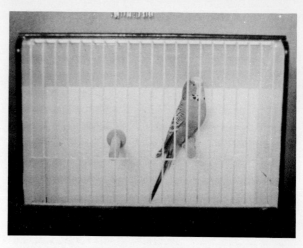

Longflight cock. Note the relative proportions of the bird and the standard show cage.

give breeders the opportunity to evaluate long flights by comparison within their own classification and so recognize the difference between good and bad specimens.

After the foregoing observations on the long flight had been written and this manuscript submitted to the publisher, further authoritative information was received from Bennett Wood, owner of Woodstock Aviaries, breeder, exhibitor, and A.B.S. panel judge. The author had seen some magnificent budgerigars of evident long flight inheritance exhibited by Mr. Wood and had learned that he had been successfully employing the mutation in his breeding endeavors for the past several years. He received an informative letter from Mr. Wood which will give the reader the benefit of knowledge derived directly from a dependable and experienced source.

Mr. Wood wrote that the mutation occurred initially about 1938 in the aviary of a non-exhibition breeder in Oxfordshire, England, who subsequently established a large stud of long flights. A well known fancier heard about the mutation and, upon arrival at the Oxfordshire aviary, found many of the birds dead and the remainder ill and suffering from malnutrition. The Oxfordshire breeder had been called into his country's service with the outbreak of war and his mother, in whose care he had left the birds, had little to feed them in that era of inflated prices. The exhibition breeder acquired those birds which survived and introduced them into his stud.

Bennett Wood goes on to say, and I quote, "After some time he (the exhibition breeder) was frightened into disposing of most of his long flights by envious exhibitors and many of them found their way indirectly into the hands of two of England's most successful exhibitors. Many of the winning birds from then on were long flights until the B.S. banned them from winning. This caused their disappearance from the show bench, but not from the breeding rooms. What took their place on the show bench were non-long flight young from long flight parents."

In answer to the author's question regarding the possibility that the long flight mutation might be the direct result of triple chromosome action,* Mr. Bennett Wood replied in his letter . . .

"I don't have the necessary knowledge of genetics to know whether this mutation resulted from the interaction of triple chromosomes instead of the normal double chromosomes, but since the long flight represents such a complete and drastic departure from the normal and this is apparently the effect triple chromosome inheritance produces, this might be the case.

"As you so aptly put it, all species have a margin of limitation for improvement beyond which limitation a mutation in the desired direction is the only answer. In the budgerigar, I'm sure the long flight is that mutation and the answer to the budgerigar breeder's prayer."

* AUTHOR'S FOOTNOTE.—There are four factors which cause change by breaking genetic equilibrium: Mutation; Selection; Migration; Genetic drift. In our controlled breeding of budgerigars we are concerned with the first two factors, not with the last two which can be replaced by a single factor pertinent to our breeding practice, namely, environment.

The phenomenon of triple chromosomes in the individual is due to chromatic change and the influenced individual is genetically labelled a triploid, signifying triple as diploid signifies the individual influenced by the usual double chromosomes, and tetraploid, a four chromosome influence, etc. An individual can have either too few chromosomes (anenploidy) or too many (polyploidy) and in some, but not all, instances the effect can be lethal. Of the two known polyploidy types, allopolyploidy and autopolyploidy, the former is the result of hybrid duplication and can radically change a species or produce a new species in one generation. Polyploidy results in larger, more vigorous individuals with a general exaggeration in structure and parts, and a need by the polyploid for an environment differing somewhat from that of the species norm. This duplication of genetic material by polyploidy could be the answer to the enigma presented by the radical mutational departure from the norm expressed by the long flight.

A lovely, young cinnamon sky hen sired by a longflight out of a normal dam.

By employing the long flight knowingly in matings to our fine normal birds, by keen selection and the application of proper breeding procedure to fix wanted long flight characteristics and eliminate the accompanying mutational faults, a better budgerigar could be evolved which would set a new and higher standard of perfection within the breed.

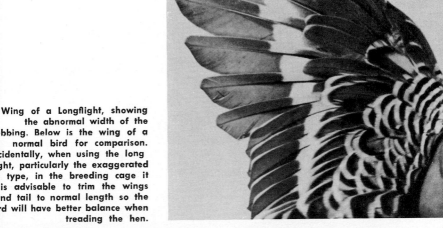

Wing of a Longflight, showing the abnormal width of the webbing. Below is the wing of a normal bird for comparison. Incidentally, when using the long flight, particularly the exaggerated type, in the breeding cage it is advisable to trim the wings and tail to normal length so the bird will have better balance when treading the hen.

Chapter 4
THE MECHANICS OF BREEDING

As many of us have been told from childhood, there is a proper time and place for everything. This is particularly true in the breeding of budgerigars. Before your pairs are put together they must be conditioned for breeding. The sexes should be provided with separate, large flights in which to strengthen and bring tone to their muscular systems. A plentiful supply of varied foods should be constantly kept before them, and they must, before being paired, display all the obvious signs of mature mating readiness. Constantly calling, strutting, displaying the bloom of excellent condition, the cocks with shiny, deep blue ceres, their beaks beating a tattoo against any solid partition in amorous eagerness, the hens with rough brown ceres, restless and calling continually to the adjacent, caged males. They are ready then to fulfill their destiny, to propagate their species.

Newly acquired birds should be given a longer period of flight cage exercise while they become acclimated to their new environment. This is particularly true of imported birds which should be allowed several months to become firmly adjusted to a new world of unaccustomed changes.

It is perhaps pertinent to mention that the colony breeding system will not be discussed here. Colony breeding is for the production of quantity not quality and only by controlled breeding can we produce better budgerigars.

THE BREEDING SEASON

When your adult birds display the amorous attitudes mentioned above, it is time to allow natural instinct to take its course. Select your pairs and put them together in their individual breeding cages. The nest box can already be in position. Unlike many other species of animals and birds, the budgerigar is not a seasonal breeder, nor is he a seasonal moulter. The best time to begin your

Two massive seven month old half-sisters from top line bred stock. Both in show and breeding cage, these two young ladies can be expected to excel.

breeding season depends upon your birds, the breeder's geographical location and the particular environment which the breeder has established for his stock. If you provide outdoor breeding accommodations it is best to begin your breeding in May when the weather has become settled and the days are longer. If your breeding is done indoors under artificial lighting and an even year-round temperature, you can put up your pairs whenever they are in breeding condition.

In England, winter breeding is frowned upon and spring breeding recommended. There is a valid reason for the English breeders to begin their breeding season in late February or early March. Much of the budgerigar breeding there is done under natural conditions without the aid of artificial light and, during the winter the days in England are much shorter than they are in the United States, thus providing much less daylight. In the budgerigar's natural habitat, Australia, which lies close to the equator, there is relatively little seasonal variation of daylight. From north to south, on that continent, the hours of light range from approximately ten to fourteen hours a day, a fact which accounts for the breed's non-seasonal breeding habits.

In our warm southern states outdoor breeding can be carried on all year round without the necessity of using artificial light or heat. In any section of the United States where birds are bred indoors there need be no specific season adhered to if enough winter warmth is provided (between 60° and 70°F.) and supplementary feeding is employed. If birds are kept in a cellar which is cool in summer, there is no reason to suspend breeding activity even during the summer months. Show-minded breeders like to make their pairings early enough to insure enough maturity in the young by fall to enable them to exhibit the youngsters in the fall shows. Fall breeding is not recommended for the exhibition fancier. He will naturally exhibit his best birds at the shows instead of using them for breeding, with the result that other, inferior birds are put up to breed which will possibly produce inferior young.

COURTING AND NESTING

Our mating pairs are in their breeding cages and the nest boxes in place. Be very sure that all perches are secure so they will not turn, move, or fall while the birds are in the act of breeding. If

A prize-winning Australian gray hen.

possible, it is best to use an experienced cock with a virgin hen or vice versa. You will notice the hen's back begin to hollow out as courting begins. Sometimes, with well conditioned pairs, breeding takes place almost immediately, but most frequently it takes a few days for the hen to acquiesce to the cock's blandishments. If the pair shows no mutual interest within a reasonable length of time and fail to go to nest, something of course, is wrong. Check the pothole in the nest box. It should be neither too large nor too small (diameter $1\frac{1}{2}$ inches). If you are using only one perch in the breeding cage try using two instead, or move one perch closer to the nest box. If the reluctant pair are red-eyes (albino or fallow) move the breeding cage to a position where there is less light. If your pair is in top breeding condition, yet all this fails, then they should be broken up or new mates respectively provided.

Allow your breeding pairs as much privacy as possible, merely tending to their basic needs, and soon the hen will be peeping into the nest box, followed shortly by complete investigation. She will begin to stay within the nest box for ever longer periods as the time of laying approaches. Do not constantly peak into the nest box to see if eggs have been laid and in so doing disturb the hen and drive her from the box. Restrain your anxiety and instead watch the hen surreptitiously when she does emerge. If she is about to lay you will see enlargement in the area of the vent. Watch her droppings also. When you see a mound of large, loose droppings you will know she has begun to lay. The hen will strip feathers from her breast for the nest and to bare her breast so greater warmth can be provided directly on the eggs. Many breeders provide fine cedar chips or shavings in the nest box to keep it dry and tidy.

If the hen lays her first eggs off the perch or throws the eggs out of the nest, replace the eggs in the nest box with agates or marbles approximately the size of an egg. Warm them in your hand first before placing them in the nest. The hen will be unable to pick them up to throw them out or, in the case of the perch-laying hen, will know then where eggs should be laid and in most instances will sit them without trouble. When subsequent eggs appear in the nest box in the normal manner the marbles can be removed.

Discreet inspection of the nest box should begin as soon as the first egg is laid. If the unfortunate occurs and a hen becomes eggbound you will then be able to give her the important immediate aid. Be sure at night, if you breed indoors, that hens with eggs or chicks in the box are not out in the breeding cage when the lights go out.

REPRODUCTION

The actual act of mating is accomplished when the hen lays over the perch, head and tail up, the cock mounts and "treads" her, balancing with one outstretched, embracing wing, he swings his tail under hers, after a bit of agitated manipulation, their cloacas touch or contact, and with typical motion the male sperm is discharged. The male reproductive organs are paired (testes) in front of the kidneys and are connected with the cloaca by a pair of thin ducts (vas deferens). In the female, the right ovary early and wholly degenerates leaving only the left ovary present. The

An exhibition English Budgie showing a set of nicely spaced, large and desirable spots. The necklace is the crowning glory of the show bird.

end of this oviduct expands to receive the ova as they burst from the oviary. The duct is glandular and albumen is secreted in the upper part, to cover the egg yolk, while the lower portion secretes the lime shell. The end opens into the cloaca as does also the excretory system.

Fertilization of the egg occurs in the upper part of the oviduct before the yolk is covered with albumen.

THE EGG

The egg consists of a large yolk, formed in the ovary, upon which a small germinal disk floats from which the embryo de-

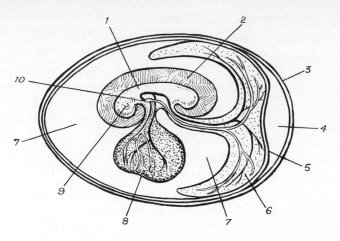

PARTS OF A FERTILE BUDGIE EGG
1. Embryo 2. Amnion 3. Outer Shell Membrane 4. Air Space 5.Inner Shell Membrane
6. Allantois 7. Albumen (Egg White) 8. Yolk Sac 9. Eye of Embryo 10. Heart
of Embryo.

velops. In passing down the upper portion of the oviduct, the yolk becomes coated with albumen (fluid egg white) which is separated from the yolk by a membrane forming an envelope for the yolk. Both yolk and albumen are used as nourishment by the developing embryo. In the lower portion of the oviduct, yolk and white are enclosed in a strong double membrane and then in a shell composed of three layers of a substance, principally calcium carbonate. The membrane layers begin to separate leaving an air space at the broad end of the egg which serves as an air reservoir from which the chick breathes as it matures in the shell.

The hen lays an egg every other day, the period of incubation varying slightly from seventeen to eighteen days. Some hens do not begin serious setting until the second egg is laid. Most cocks take up their solitary vigil on the nest-box perch, occasionally peeking through the pot hole or feeding the expectant mother hen. Occasionally, a cock will aid his hen sit the eggs and spend almost as much time in the nest box as she does.

A few days after laying a change will be noticed in fertile eggs. They will begin to turn from a fragile, whitish tan to dull, full white as they become more occluded by the development of the inner embryo. Those which remain whitish tan are not fertile, but don't be too hasty in casting them out. Eggs which, after a time, exhibit a leaden, darker grey tone contain either dead-in-shell chicks or only partially developed dead embryos. If the season is particularly dry, eggs can become dried and the developing chicks in the shell die. A piece of blotting paper soaked with water should be put under the nest-box block, with the end of the blotter projecting to be used as a wick for more water as the occasion arises, to alleviate dryness.

Failure of eggs to hatch may be caused by a number of things, among them, infertility of either parent, hen being disturbed so that she sits erratically or allows eggs to get cold, careless handling of eggs, wet nests (diarrhea or wet feeders), vermin, lack of essential nutritional elements for embryonic growth within the egg, etc. Loose perches are also a prime cause of infertile eggs.

Newly hatched chicks are nearly impossible to evaluate except for obvious cripples.

When the chick is ready to leave the egg it will begin peeping and then chipping at the inside shell wall with its tiny beak, cutting a circle in the center diameter of the shell until it parts into two halves. The chick emerges free, tiny, nude, blind, and helpless. At this time a small amount of fine cedar shavings can be put in the nest box to absorb the moisture of the chick's excretia and keep the nest box block clean and dry. The shavings can be changed every few days. If they are of cedar, they will also aid in eliminating mite infestation in the nest box.

When hatching begins, the young should be quietly examined daily. Be sure the parents or feeder pair are adequately feeding their poults. If they are not, then the chicks must be put under another pair. The parental instinct in budgerigars is highly developed, probably aided by the bird's lack of ability to discriminate by scent, for in most instances, pairs will usually adopt youngsters other than their own without fuss.

A cup filled with seed can be attached to the inside of the nest box for the hen sitting on a clutch of eggs or with hatched young. This arrangement is advantageous if the hen "goes thin" during the process of laying, hatching and feeding the clutch. Yet it is not a practice the author particularly advocates since the hen, during this period, is not burning up energy through activity and she needs the bit of exercise and change she gets from leaving the nest box to feed in the breeding cage.

One can firmly attach an auxiliary feeding cup inside the nest box when the chicks are from two and a half to three weeks old. This helps the babies to learn more quickly to crack and eat seeds and so be conditioned to leave the nest box for the freedom of the breeding cage at an earlier age than usual. They can be taken from the breeding box and put into the breeding cage as soon as the belly-down has fairly well closed, at approximately twenty-eight days of age. Most breeders allow the chicks to remain in the nesting box until they emerge of their own accord. Ancestral instinct keeps the poults from emerging until they are able to cope with the dangers that beset all helpless young in the wild state, but under domestic conditions, predatory dangers are eliminated and the emergence time can be shortened.

This is sound practice, but only if the cock sire is a good feeder and both parents are amiable toward the young in the breeding

Chicks from top Scottish breeding with foster parents, a pair of feeders that will keep their crops full and tend them well so they will emerge from the nest as big, strong and smoothly feathered chicks.

cage. If the cock feeds the released chicks well and they themselves have learned to eat seeds early, the drop in growth which occurs when the chick is transferred to a flight cage is greatly lessened. But if a hen (usually a young hen with her first clutch) refuses to feed her newly hatched chick, remove the baby, placing him in another nest box where there are well-cared-for young. Replace the newly hatched chick with a poult five or six days old. The older chick will demand food from the hen and will get it. After two or three days the hen has formed the habit of feeding and her own youngster can then be safely returned to her.

FOSTER PARENTS

"Feeder" pairs, or foster parents, are put together at the same time you mate your quality breeders so that they will begin laying at approximately parallel times. When both clutches are completed, the eggs of the feeder pair are disposed of and replaced by the eggs from the choice pair of breeders. The latter eggs should be marked with color to differentiate them from any further eggs the feeder pair may lay. Before putting the substitute eggs in the feeders' nest box, warm them well in your hands for hens will, not infrequently, cast out or refuse to sit cold eggs.

The choice breeding pair from whom you have removed the eggs will breed and go to nest again in from two-and-a-half to three weeks time. By using the foster-parent method, it is possible to take as many as four clutches of eggs from a fully mature, well-fed and conditioned hen instead of the generally recommended two clutches since she is not feeding young and therefore not draining her strength to any great degree. It is not in the *hen's* best interest to do this, however. She will be spending too much time confined to the small breeding cage. There is always the possibility of egg-binding occurring during the laying of that third or fourth clutch. One must also consider that, if the same cock is used to father the hen's four clutches, he is draining himself by feeding the hen while she is in the nest.

It is a good plan to allow your choice pair to hatch and feed two or three youngsters from the last clutch, if they will feed well, so they can become accustomed to the rigors of parenthood.

To have success with the foster-parent method, these feeder pairs must of necessity be heavy feeders. The crop of a well fed chick will obviously exhibit fullness and appear mealy yellow in contrast to the body pinkness. As they grow, their underparts should be all crop and belly and feel soft and flaccid to the touch. Foster parents should not be allowed to raise more than three or four young if these chicks are to receive full nutritional benefits and reach maximum size. It is best, if possible, to split the clutches from your quality pairs, distributing the eggs between two feeder nests instead of one. In this way, should accident occur in one nest which causes loss of the eggs or the young, you will still have some of the important results of the mating in another nest. All this could have been more simply said by merely admonishing you "not to put all your eggs in one basket."

CHANGING MATES

Should you wish to alter your breeding combinations and, after removing the hen's eggs to feeder nests, breed her to a different male, it is best to remove the nest box or block the entrance hole with a stiff piece of cardboard, then introduce the newly selected mate. Do not allow the pair freedom of the nest box for several days, or until you are sure, by their actions, that the hen has accepted her new spouse and harmony reigns in the breeding cage.

If a particularly prepotent cock is to be used with several different hens it is best to change him immediately from one hen to the next. If there is any lapse of time between the changes he will go into an after-breeding moult and you will have to wait until he is fully feathered and fit before using him again. No cock should be forced to spend months on end in breeding cages. The bird himself will of course not complain, which is the nature of the male of any species, but he should be given a vacation in the male flight to stretch his wings and regain vigor before resuming his duties in the breeding cage.

CROP MILK

The crop milk with which the budgerigar feeds its young is surely one of Mother Nature's most wonderful inventions. It is rich in all the nutritional elements needed for the proper growth and development of the chicks in the nest, a thirty-day period of almost explosive growth in the young.

This colostrum-like crop milk, actually processed in the proventriculus, or stomach, is a form of milk curd received from the protein and fat-rich cells which form the inner lining of the proventriculus and gullet in ever-increasing number and thickness during the period of egg incubation. These highly nutritious cells break away as the eggs hatch, mix with digestive juices, pepsin, a digestive enzyme from the proventriculus, secretions from the mucous glands, and stomach oil, and the end result is regurgitated and fed to the young. This "milk" is rich in vitamins and minerals (particularly lecithin and vitamin A) which accompany the exclusive fat and protein content, but lacks the starches (carbohydrates) which are so abundant in the staple seed diet. Since starches are not present but fat and protein are, it necessarily follows that the birds, to manufacture this crop milk, must synthesize the necessary elements by robbing their own bodies and tissues. Supplements rich in the necessary nutritive elements, particularly protein, must be fed during this period of crop-milk manufacture. This subject will be discussed more completely in the chapter on feeding (Chapter 6).

In the first days of the chick's life the crop milk fed is quite liquid and high in fat content. As the poults grow the milk becomes thicker in consistency, more solid, and the fat content decreases to some extent, while the protein increases. It is interesting to observe that the crop milk fed to the youngest chick in a nest is more liquid than that which is regurgitated for the accommodation of the older chicks.

CARELESS FEEDERS

Some parents are careless feeders, smearing crop milk over the beaks and faces of the young. This residue has a tendency to harden and can cause malformation of the upper mandible which in the young is pliable and tender. For this reason the chicks of known careless feeders should be checked daily and, if necessary, residue food adhering to the beak should be carefully cleaned away. Check also the feet and legs of the babies which sometimes become balled with hardened feces. Should this occur, soak and loosen the adhering matter in warm water and remove gently.

BANDING

There are various ways of holding the chick during the process of banding and at least two recommended ways of banding. The vital consideration is to get the band on without injuring the chick. The correct age to band varies with the size of the chick, particularly the size of its feet and legs. Some youngsters of particularly big English stock require banding at four or five days of age. Others, from smaller stock, will not retain the band on their legs before they are six or seven days old. When the opening eye slit

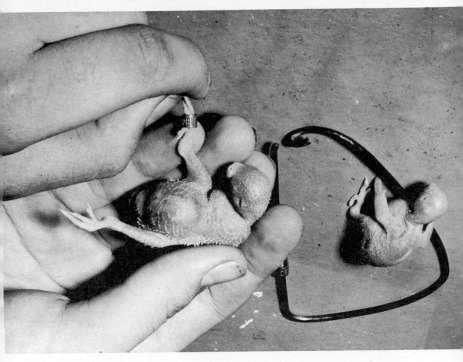

Banding a Budgie chick. This is the first step; slipping the band over the two forward (or three) toes. The small, inside toe has not yet been pulled through the ring. The piece of heavy wire is used to hold the bands.

of normal sized birds just begins to show, it is generally the proper time to band.

When banding hold the chick in the left hand, belly up and head toward you. With the fingers of the left hand hold the baby's right foot and leg and slip the band, held in your right hand, over the two forward toes. Then push the band up as close to the elbow as possible. The short and long rear toes will be imprisoned beneath the band and the band must be pushed up far enough on the leg to allow the fork between these two toes to show. With a sharpened stick first pull the short toe out from under the band, then the long rear toe, and the job is done! This is not the only way to band, but it is the method the author uses and has found easy to accomplish.

The stick used should not be too sharply pointed at the immediate end or it might cause injury. Some breeders pull three

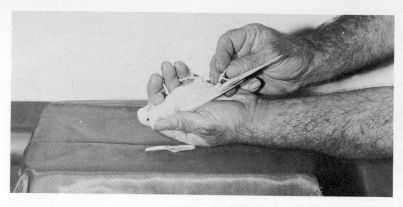

Even a full-sized bird can easily be banded with the identifying plastic family band.

toes through the band and then, with the sharpened stick, free the remaining toe. Should you, for any reason, allow the chick to become too old for easy banding, a bit of vaseline applied to the chick's leg or the inside of the band will aid in the operation. The gaily colored family bands, split in the center, are easily applied at any age, but should really be put on when the youngster is taken from the parents and put in the nursery flight. It is easy then, by a glance at the band color, and without handling the bird, to be able to check its origin.

PEDIGREES AND RECORDS

The pedigree of a purchased budgerigar is not generally an accurate measurement of his breeding worth. It is merely a record of ancestry. The records and pedigrees which you will compile are the ones which will be of value. For it is of the utmost importance to record the faults that are carried by your breeding lines as well as the virtues, and this information you will not find on the usual pedigree.

The pedigree card should include the bird's color, individual band number, sex, date of hatching, family band color, and a three generation pedigree of his ancestry, with color variety, breeder, and number of each of his forbears.

A complete set of records should be kept of each individual bird and every breeding made. A loose-leaf notebook serves admirably as a breeding register. Here is a sample breeding register page.

Breeding Compartment No. 4

VIOLET/CINNAMON COCK.   CINNAMON SKY HEN
         22-441H-'59   44-441H-'59
    Began Clutch-3/10/'60   Due-3/28/'60
         Began Hatching-3/28/'60
    Eggs-(6)   Hatched-(5)   Reared-(5)
         Banded-61, 62, 63, 64, 65.
    Family Band-Blue and Yellow
         (100% English breeding)

REMARKS-One egg infertile. Pair allowed to
  hatch and rear two chicks and are good
  feeders. Other three eggs fostered out to
  Feeder Pair #4. (Lt. Green Cock & Yellow Hen)
  Chicks large, vigorous, good heads.

Sex and Color-Violet/Cinnamon Cock #61
  Cinnamon Cobalt Cock #62-Cinnamon Sky
  Violet Hen #63-Cinnamon Cobalt Hen #64
  Violet Hen #65.

The nest boxes attached to your breeding compartments should be numbered and this number employed in the breeding register.

On the breeding cage or the nest box, a small filing card or tag should be attached with the following information: Breeding pair and band numbers, when clutch was begun, when due, when hatched, number of eggs laid, number hatched, band number of chicks and family band color.

Individual records can be typed or written on a filing card and filed in either band order rotation, by family or color variety whichever the breeder prefers. This card can be similar to the one depicted below:

The opposite side of this card is the most important, for here we find a rating given to each of the basic elements of structure and color and, of even more worth, a record of the genetic traits we know this individual bird to possess from both the progeny test and ancestry.

SIZE: E (large) COLOR: E+ MARKINGS: E+
SUBSTANCE: E POSTURE: E BACK: G+
(slight saddle dip) HEAD: E-
(Lacks slightly in frontal forward arch)
MASK: E (Excellent depth) SPOTS: G+
(well spaced, could be slightly larger)-
WING CARRIAGE: E.   TAIL CARRIAGE: E.
TEMPERAMENT: E+ (quiet, not flighty)
          OVERALL RATING: E
REMARKS: Carries recessive for slight lack of
   backskull and tendency to be high in rump
   (with dropped tail).

We have thus a complete and accurate picture of the individual bird, and the breeding worth of every budgerigar in our possession.

A small finishing nail should be tacked to the outside of the nest box. When you are fairly sure of the number of fertile eggs in the nest, count out a similar number of bands (both number and family bands) and hang them on the brad with a piece of string. In this way youngsters from each nest will be banded in sequence.

Incidentally, lately the author has been trimming the vent feathers of both hens and cocks to assure fertility. Sometimes these feathers, particularly in the hen, fold over the cloaca, blocking it to the male's sperm. I also, in the morning when I am feeding the birds their supplementary protein food, rouse sitting hens from the nest box out into the breeding cage with the cock, then block the pot hole so that they cannot immediately return to the nest box. Generally this gives the cock time to breed the hen and fertilize the coming eggs. Infertile eggs are often caused by cocks lacking the opportunity to properly breed the hens because they do not emerge often and long enough to be bred. Never block the hole for more than a few minutes or the eggs already laid may get chilled. Once the full complement of eggs are in the nest this practice should be discontinued.

ENDING BREEDING

There are several methods used to end the breeding efforts of a pair of budgerigars. One easy way is to remove any eggs laid while the pair were finishing feeding the last clutch of youngsters, and return the birds to their respective flights. If no eggs have been laid by the time the last hatched chicks are out of the nest box, simply remove the nest box and allow the parents a few more days of feeding the young before breaking them up. Another method is to remove the cock before the pair begin mating again and allow the hen to finish feeding the present clutch.

If enough feeder pairs are put to nest, many breeding-cage disasters can be overcome. Sometimes we find that one of a pair will savage the young or kill them. Some hens, and occasionally cocks, are feather pluckers, some break eggs consistently and, occasionally, one of a breeding pair dies while there are young in the nest. Of course, birds which kill or maim their young or break eggs should be instantly banished from your breeding stock. If some of the chicks are to be saved, the advantage of foster parents is obvious. These youngsters though, when mature, must be test-mated to be sure that they have not inherited any of their parents' deplorable habits. When one parent dies, the other parent often will take over the duties of rearing the chicks. But it is best to foster the chicks to feeder pairs if possible rather than relying on a single parent taking over, especially if the survivor is the male.

Chapter 5
AVIARIES AND EQUIPMENT

The facilities the breeder has at his disposal for his hobby as well as the climate in which he lives varies so greatly that no hard and fast rules can be laid down for the construction of living and breeding facilities for his birds. In this chapter we can only deal in generalities due to these conditions. In the southern states outdoor facilities can be utilized throughout the year. In the northern states outdoor flights are only useful during the warmer months. Many earnest breeders use a room in their home or apartment, a cellar or attic, and through earnest endeavor and a knowledgeable approach, breed quality stock. Aviaries can be beautiful, incorporating individual touches of design, or they can be plain and strictly functional, depending upon the inner urge of the owner. We will disregard the aesthetic and concentrate on the purely functional aspects since beauty lies in the eye of the beholder and that which is lovely to one individual may appear ornate and without specific purpose to another.

FLIGHTS

The aviary should be equipped with a minimum of three flights, one for cocks, one for hens, and one to serve as a nursery flight. If possible a youth or adolescent flight and a flight for culled birds which are to be disposed of should be added to this total. If these flights are indoors it is convenient to have them high enough so that the breeder can step inside without having to crouch. The same is true of outdoor flights, but we assume that the height of outdoor flights will be adequate for this purpose.

Flights for grown birds should be at least $4\frac{1}{2}$ feet long, 3 feet deep and 3 feet high. Actually a good rule-of-thumb to use in constructing a flight is that, within reason, they cannot be too long. If the flight is not high enough to step into, it should be raised from the floor on legs and should have a removable front for easy cleaning. The back of indoor flights should be a solid

An inexpensive indoor flight which you can walk into.

partition of either plywood or masonite enamelled white. The top, two sides and front should be of wire. For these raised, smaller flights a wire bottom above the two or three metal trays (number of trays in relation to length) will allow hulls and feces to drop through to the trays.

The wire used on all flights differs with the personal opinion of the breeder. Some advocate half-inch square wire, others one-half by one inch wire and still others, quarter-inch hardware cloth. The latter gives poor visibility into the flight, but is perhaps the most functional since it will keep mice out of the flight cages. If painted with a non-toxic black paint, the visibility improves to a great extent.

Perches should be placed at each end of the flight in stair formation, placed far enough apart so that the budgerigar's tails do not rub or catch upon the perch above. They should vary in thickness from one quarter-inch to one half-inch in diameter. They can be attached at either end to a solid strip of wood, and the whole mounted as a unit at one end of the flight.

In the smaller, indoor flights, there should be at least two doors at each side of the front, big enough to admit a catching net without trouble. A door opening out and upward in the middle of the front with a tray rigidly constructed inside the flight, can be utilized to advantage in feeding dishes of supplements.

In outdoor flights only one, full sized door is needed which should open inward. It is best to fashion a small safety entrance so that any birds, escaping from the flight will be trapped here and easily caught and returned. Though most outdoor flights are constructed with wire ceilings it is by far better to use a solid ceiling eliminating the worry of wild birds landing and defecating into the flight and bringing disease or parasites to your birds. For the same reason it is best to use double wire for the enclosure of the flights. If two-by-threes or fours are used as structural members for the flights, wire can be stretched on the outside of the two-by-three and a second, inner stretch of wire attached to the inner side of the two-by-three. Wild birds clinging to the outer wire cannot then come in direct contact with your budgerigars. The roof will not keep sunlight from the inside of the flight, since at certain hours it will slant its rays in to cover a good deal of the inner flight.

Floors for outdoor flights can be made of cement, slightly slanted for drainage when hosed off. Or, a drain can be built into the floor to serve the same purpose. Soil-cement is less expensive than true cement and will serve your purpose well. This is the subsurface employed on light-traffic airfields and many suburban roads. The area to be surfaced is dug up to a depth of about four inches, the soil pulverized and dry cement, in a ratio of two-thirds of a sack of cement to a square yard of surface, is thoroughly mixed into the pulverized soil. A mist spray is then hosed onto the surface, it is raked to full depth to insure uniform moisture, and then leveled, followed by tamping for compactness and then rolling with a garden roller. After rolling it is mist-sprayed again and covered with a layer of sawdust for about a week. After that it is ready for use.

FLIGHT EQUIPMENT

In the nursery flight it is best to use shallow pans for food so that the youngsters will have no difficulty in finding adequate nourishment. In the youth flights, both shallow pans and hoppers should be used to allow the youngsters time to become accustomed to eating from the hoppers. But, in the grown bird flights, the most convenient receptacles for feeding seeds are hoppers. If possible they should be designed with the husk drawers removable from the back of the hopper. They can then be so situated in the flight that they can be cleaned or filled from the outside. If the drawer pulls out to the front, the hopper can be mounted on a door which opens outward.

Next to an automatic watering system, the best way to provide water in your flights is by using one or two outside water bottles held to the flight side by clamps and possessing a large flange into which the bottle is set and which juts through the wire into the flight. The water supply is not so easily fouled by the birds with this arrangement. These are quite similar to the smaller, tube waterers but are made in flight size. If the flight is very large and houses a great number of birds the large, fountain-type waterers can be used.

Clamps attached to the sides of the flight can be utilized to hold cuttlebone or a substitute and greens. Receptacles for grit can be placed on the inside trays which may also be used for supplements.

BREEDING CAGES

Though flights cannot be too large (within reason), contrary to accepted belief, breeding cages cannot be too small (within reason). Many breeders, particularly in England, use large, box-like breeding cages with the nest box inside. With this arrangement it is awkward examining the nests. The basic reason for the breeding cage is obviously, for the birds to breed and when the cage is too large they will not ordinarily breed as quickly as when the cage is small and they are in close proximity. Double breeder canary cages with the middle partition removed making a breeding cage 20 inches long, by 10 inches high and 11 inches deep, serve as ideal breeding cages for budgerigars. A good size is also 18 inches long, 14 inches high and 10 inches deep. The latter is an all-metal cage used by the author, enclosed on three sides and fashioned to stack into any size units.

The birds do not have flight space in these small breeding cages, but since they spend only a limited time in them and then are

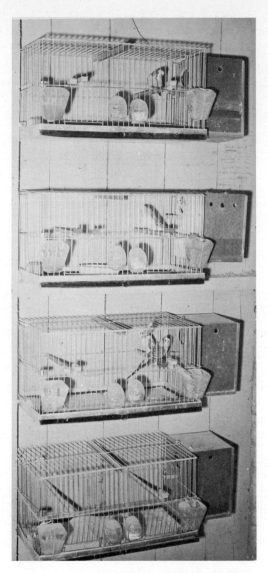

A group of indoor breeding cages in use. Note the plastic, pear-shaped seed and water containers. This type of open cage is used by many fanciers in this country. It is actually a double compartment canary breeding cage with the middle partition removed.

released into the larger flight cages, this does them no harm. If they feel in need of wing exercise, they will fly in one place, above the perch, or hang onto the perch and flap their wings at a terrific rate of speed. The hens feel more comfortable in the smaller cages, for when they have young in the nest they dislike getting very far away from them and also, in the smaller cage food and water are close by.

Two perches, securely fastened, are maximum for the breeding cage. Many breeders prefer one perch with the nest box perch serving as the second perch. A low perch is generally placed along the cage front to make the food containers more approachable, and it is amazing how often budgerigars will use this perch on which to mate in preference to the higher perches.

Breeding cages of the sizes recommended can be easily built, if need be, out of plywood and ready-made fronts bought for them. Naturally, with breeding cages as small as these, the nest box is attached outside the cage which makes it easily accessible for cleaning and examination of eggs or chicks.

Double trays on the bottom, employing a wire mesh tray on top for the droppings to fall through, and a solid underneath tray to catch the droppings, are not particularly good in a breeding cage. When the young are beginning to leave the nest and fly into the breeding cage, it is prudent to scatter seeds over the cage floor and to fill shallow jar tops with soaked seed and supplement for the babies. With the wire tray arrangement, seeds cannot be scattered. Due to the young chick's clumsy feeding habits, much of the tray food will be lost through the wire mesh.

Tube waterers are handy for the breeding cage but they must be large enough to hold water for at least two days, for breeding pairs with young in the nest consume a great deal of water. Pearshaped seed cups, made of clear plastic and cleverly fashioned like small, individual hoppers are the best vehicle for furnishing seeds in the breeding cage. They attach outside the cage and have a small flap on top into which seed is poured. A similar cup is made for water without the top flap and is so fashioned as to keep the drinking water from becoming fouled. These pearshaped drinkers are extremely serviceable and can be used in place of the tube waterers. The same type of holder used for seeds can be utilized for grit, or a smaller, canary glass cup can be used.

Holders of the clip variety can be purchased for holding greens. Cuttlebone generally comes with holder attached and so do the calcium and mineral blocks sold commercially. An open plastic cup which attaches to the cage bars near the perch can be used for supplements, wet or dry. If used for dry supplement, the small treat cups which are pushed between the cage bars, can be filled with wet supplement, two or three at a time, for each breeding cage with young in the nest.

NEST BOXES

The best kind of nest boxes to use is the type illustrated. They are generally made of either all plywood or with doors of masonite. The wider box has the advantage of greater space to which the

The common type of nest box.

E.H.HART

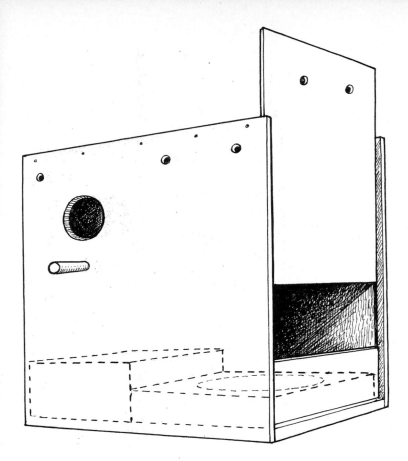

The special type of nest box, larger than the common type, with the egg block situated away from the pot-hole and entrance.

hen can retire when the young in the nest are getting too large and demanding. She can also shove the young into the other section near the pothole when she is laying a second clutch. Both the large and smaller section at the bottom on the door side slide up but only the door is used in this manner and the bottom section keeps the young from falling out during examination. The bottom section is raised when nest blocks are to be removed.

The exit holes are off center, not because the hen or cock will break eggs by coming down directly onto them, I have never seen this actually happen, but so that the young, clumsy chicks, going

A young cobalt cock of excellent breeding.

On the facing page are a lovely pair of adolescent Harlequins or recessive Pieds. This photo illustrates the two basic colors, Blue and Green, as they are affected by the recessive Pied pattern.

in and out of the box, will not break second clutch eggs as they descend into the nest box. Nest boxes should not be too shallow in depth, for this makes it too easy for vigorous, inquisitive chicks to leave the nest box too early.

TWO FLOOR PLANS FOR COMBINED AVIARIES AND BREEDING QUARTERS

SCALE ¼ IN. = 1 FT.

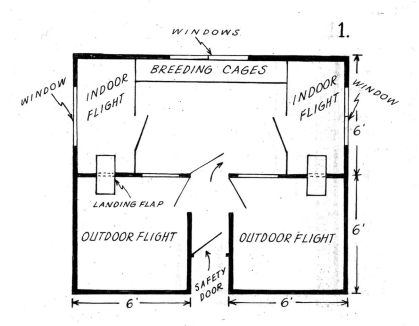

1.

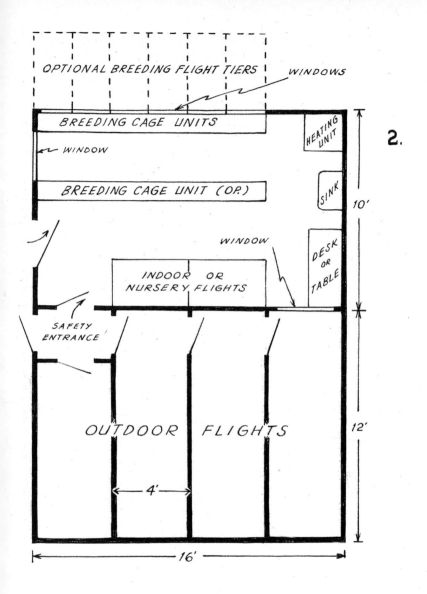

OPTIONAL BREEDING FLIGHT TIERS

WINDOWS

2.

BREEDING CAGE UNITS

HEATING UNIT

WINDOW

SINK

BREEDING CAGE UNIT (OP.)

10'

WINDOW

DESK OR TABLE

INDOOR OR NURSERY FLIGHTS

SAFETY ENTRANCE

OUTDOOR FLIGHTS

12'

4'

16'

The illustrations of aviary floor plans are simply to provide a basis from which to work, for just as each man likes his own home to mirror to some extent his own personality and wants, so each breeder likes to plan his aviary to fit his own needs.

A huge young cinnamon green cock of English breeding. Note the size of the
feet of this bird.

Mauve opaline, a two dark factor bird in the blue series. The opaline factor is variable and careful, early selective breeding must be carried out to improve the strain. With the knowledge of genetics, the Budgie breeder automatically knows that this bird carries two factors for opaline and two dark factors. The condition of the two "like" factors is termed "homozygous." If the bird should be split for another factor, it would be called "heterozygous."

GENERAL EQUIPMENT

A hospital cage is necessary in any well equipped aviary. One can be bought or made. To make a hospital cage, use metal preferably for the three sides and top, with holes or open spaces along the top for ventilation. A false bottom is built into which two bulb sockets are fitted with an outside switch, the whole section lined with asbestos material. A thermometer is hung inside and two perches are attached with facilities for food and water containers easily available to the bird. The front section of glass should slide up readily to serve as a door. A wire mesh tray should be fixed above the bottom tray which is directly above the false, completely enclosed heating compartment.

For general cleaning a paint scraper is handy for cleaning trays and a perch brush, or sandpaper for perches. A hand brush can be used for general cage cleaning and a small, slender, stiff brush for water tubes and assorted cups. A broom and shovel is automatically part of your cleaning equipment. A vacuum cleaner will be of immeasurable aid in cleaning up feathers and seed hulls on the floor and the many attachments can be used for flight and even cage cleaning, sucking up husks and other debris in short order.

A large garbage can with a closely fitting cover is admirable for storing seed. A smaller 5 or 10 pound can kept separately can be used if seed is treated with feeding oil. A desk is a handy piece of equipment to have in the breeding room, for here records can be kept and when necessary, quickly checked against the birds at hand.

Mite sprays and powder, disinfectant, iodine, Merthiolate, one-inch gauze bandage, scissors, medicine droppers and tweezers, should be kept in the medicine cabinet or box. Tools should be handy as well as one or two catching nets and an extra nest block for every nest box to make exchange easy.

Chapter 6

FEEDING AND MANAGEMENT

Over the years breeders of budgerigars have fed a standard, staple and static diet to their birds, consisting of canary, millet and some oat seeds, occasionally greens, grit, cuttlebone and water. To this basic diet many knowing breeders now add various supplementary mixtures; many have special formulas which they swear by. As we shall see, supplementary feeding is a necessity if vigorous, large, better budgerigars is your breeding aim.

Diet, to be effective, must be complete and balanced in the nutritional elements necessary to a particular species. No really progressive, scientific research has been done to determine the nutritional needs of budgerigars, because animals in the pet and hobby field have no economic value in a national sense. Lacking this pertinent knowledge, breeders who realize the need for supplementary feeding, mix their own dietary formulas in an earnest effort to provide missing dietary essentials. But, without a basic knowledge of what those essential needs are, the result must necessarily be a hit-and-miss effort, with emphasis on the *miss*.

We must first understand the physiology of the budgerigar to know how best he can be fed. Like all birds, the budgerigar exhibits a higher body temperature than that of other animals; his breathing is faster, too. These two peculiarities alone are an index of the intense activity of the bird's life in general, flying vigorously and, in the case of the wild budgerigar, migrating from one feeding ground to the next and spending a good deal of time on the ground moving about in search of food. Budgerigars lack teeth with which to grind their food. They possess large crops which secrete crop milk for the feeding of their young, and the glandular part of the stomach is small in common with all birds that feed primarily on grains and seeds. The basic nutritional needs of the budgerigar must supply the material for growth,

A young, green long flight, clearly exhibiting the characteristics of the basic, long flight mutation.

If Circular Crested Normal Cobalt. Good or and markings. Crest o small. Lacks in spots.

Halfsider Recessive Pied Cobalt. Exhibits 5 clearly defined colors. A mutation rarely occurring in this combination.

Dutch Pied Clearflight Light Green. Fairly good in type but lacks in skull and spots. Yellow reaches too far down.

fted Normal Skyblue. r in shape, size and est. Color very patchy, ks spots. Markings not clearly defined.

Quartersider Opaline Dark Green-Cobalt. Another unusual, not inheritable, color combination. A well shaped, good sized bird.

Australian Banded Pied Normal Green. Good in color, type and band. Pure, light wings. Lacks size in body, spots, and head.

feather production, energy, crop milk and a supplement to assist in grinding the food intake. Since budgies eat only the seed kernel and discard the husk, cellulose must be supplied by some other means.

BASIC NUTRITIONAL ESSENTIALS

Dietary Essentials and *Natural Sources*

1. PROTEIN: Eggs, meat, soybeans, dairy products.
2. FAT: Butter, milk, oils, cream, oil seeds.
3. CARBOHYDRATES: Canary and millet seeds, cereals, vegetables, honey.
4. VITAMIN A: Greens, peas, eggs, milk, beans, asparagus.
5. THIAMINE: Vegetables, legumes, eggs, muscle meat, milk, yeast, whole grains.
6. RIBOFLAVIN: Milk, egg yolk, wheat germ, yeast, beef, chicken, green leaves, cottonseed meal, liver.
7. NIACIN: Milk, liver, yeast, lean meat.
8. VITAMIN D: Fortified milk, eggs, fish liver oils.
9. ASCORBIC ACID: Raw cabbage, tomatoes, citrus fruits.
10. IRON, CALCIUM, PHOSPHORUS: Milk, eggs, soybeans, oatmeal, bone marrow, vegetables, liver, green-ground bonemeal.

Any substance may be considered food which can be utilized as a body-building material, a source of energy or a regulator of body activity. Seeds, greens, grit, cuttlebone and water alone do not fill these needs adequately as can be seen by the list of necessary ingredients above.

The basic nutritional needs are supplied by the three dietary essentials, proteins, fats and carbohydrates. Proteins build new body tissue and are composed of amino acids, which differ in combination with the various proteins. Carbohydrates furnish the fuel for body building and energy. Fat produces heat which becomes energy. Vitamins and minerals, in general, act as regulators of cell activity. Proteins are essentially the basic materials of life, for living cells are composed of protein molecules.

The seeds which we feed our birds have an abundance of carbohydrates which supply budgerigars with the energy necessary for their active life. But seeds sadly lack proteins and canary and millet seeds have little fat content. Oats are higher in fats but lack sufficient protein and vital vitamins and minerals, as do canary and millet seeds. Greens, fresh bark, and various kinds of wood supply the necessary cellulose the budgie discards in the shucked seed hulls. Grit supplies the element necessary to grind the swallowed food in the gizzard to a consistency which can be easily digested. There are several commercially blended grits which also contain many minerals necessary to bird health. Cuttlebone supplies necessary calcium and phosphorus for the building of bone and egg shell elements.

The important dietary essentials lacking in the basic diet (seeds, greens, grit, cuttlebone and water) are the elements which produce: 1, feathers; 2, growth, through the building of new body tissue; 3, the ingredients that constitute crop milk which must sustain and nourish the young during that first important month of explosive growth. It can be readily seen that two of the three basic nutritional needs, proteins and fats, which supply the important dietary essentials, and the vitamins and minerals which accompany these essentials, must be supplied by supplementary feeding.

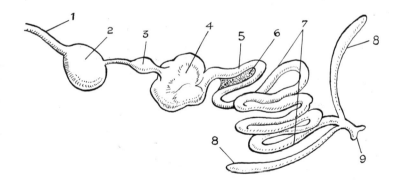

THE DIGESTIVE SYSTEM OF THE BUDGERIGAR
1. Gullet 2. Crop 3. Glandular Stomach 4. Gizzard 5. Duodenum 6. Pancreas
7. Intestine 8. Coeca 9. Cloaca

Many hobbyists will argue that in the wild state the budgerigar is not supplied with a supplementary diet yet survives, reproduces, grows and flourishes. This argument is valid but based on a false assumption. The wild bird is not the budgerigar we breed in our

Fallow Light Green. Good color and markings. Lacks type and size badly. Head and spots much too small.

Fallow Cobalt. Good color and markings but bad type. Too small, bad head with protruding beak, lacking in spots.

Crested Normal Cob (With neck mane). Rar seen visible expression 2 inheritable factors Crested. A new varie

Dark-eyed Clear White. Combination of dominant and recessive Pied factors. Good color but small in body. Tail droops so stance incorrect.

Lutino. Good size and excellent color. Slightly heavy, hence faulty stance. Good large head but lacks frontal in this shot.

Tufted Normal Dark Gre Good size, color and ty Good crest but skull la width. Spots too sm and irregu

Above, hanging boxes in a colony-breeding aviary. The photo below illustrates a type of nest box used much more frequently in England and Scotland than in the United States.

aviaries. In the wild state the budgerigar has many more foods to choose from, foods that supply a greater range of food essentials, including proteins. This greater nutritional scope is particularly suited to the wild budgerigar's metabolism since they are native to its habitat. Nature's stark "survival of the fittest" law is grimly at work in the wild state, eliminating all birds unable to survive and propagate in their native environment.

Compare this natural selection and environment to that which is fostered upon our aviary birds. Our imposed selection is opposite to natural selection. We select for larger size, bigger heads and greater substance, producing a bird which could never compete with its small, swift, fast-flying wild relatives in escaping from natural enemies, competing for food or flying great distances to more bountiful feeding grounds. In our search for type we are apt to overlook elementary essentials, such as fertility and the marked ability of a budgerigar to rear and feed its progeny.

All these abilities are necessary for survival in the wild, but for unnumbered generations we have supplied a completely artificial environment for our budgerigars. This has undoubtedly effected changes in the domestic breed's metabolism. Unlike man, who can improvise and invent to fit his environment, animals must capitulate to their environment or die. Small mutations undoubtedly occur acclimating the bird to the unnatural environment domesticity has brought. These mutations become established by selection and would not occur under natural conditions. The budgerigars which possess them survive and flourish, those which do not gradually succumb until, after many generations have passed, a breed exists in the domestic state which has different needs than its wild ancestors.

SEEDS

Canary and millet are the two types of seeds which form the basic seed diet fed our domesticated budgerigars. Mixture percentages may vary with the ideas of the individual breeder, but an approximate 50-50 blend of the two varieties is good. For baby budgies a mixture which contains a greater percentage of canary to millet is best for the simple reason that canary is easier to crack and thus the chick will consume more food over a given period.

Head study of a young Sky cock. Note the solid thickness and rise of the frontal, the overhang in front over the cere and over the eyes forming a pronounced brow. Observe the height over the eyes and the rounded sweep into the backskull. Huge, well-spaced spots and the evident proud stance would make this bird outstanding anywhere. This is the kind of head that wins the awards in England . . . and anyplace else where Budgies are shown.

Recessive Pied Mauve. Good size, type, color and markings for this difficult-to-breed variety.

Dominant Dutch Pied Olive Green. Shows similarity to recessive Pieds in this specimen. Lacks back skull, drooping tail.

Australian Dominant Pied Opaline Grey Green. Big bird of good type, color, spots, and head qualities. Dark tail faulty.

Recessive Yellow Face Blue (Type I). Nice color and markings. Blue could be more extensive. Head small, lacks back skull.

Recessive Pied Skyblue. Nice color and markings, but too small in body and head for exhibition bird.

Australian Pied Whiteflight Cobalt. Evenly marked, good color and type. Throat spots uneven.

White and yellow-face opaline cocks. The yellow-face is split to clearwing and, when mated to his companion's white sister, will produce some rainbows.

Both types of seed should be large, plump, and shiny. Imported seeds are the best. Imported Italian white millet is the finest millet, large and soft-shelled with a large, meaty kernel. Domestic Proso millet is good and widely used in this country. Millet should be selected for large size, creamy-white color, soft shell and large kernel. *Do not use the red or small, dark varieties of millet.*

Canary seed that is imported is far superior to the domestic seed and is the variety used most extensively by breeders. Seeds can also be planted and the sprouts are relished by the birds.

A 5 to 10 per cent quantity of hulled oats (outer shells removed) is a wise addition to the seed diet. Most budgies will eat the oats in the mixture before they devour the other seeds. For this reason many breeders advocate a separate feeding of oats. Actually it makes little difference whether oats are fed separately or in the seed mix; once the birds have disposed of the oats, they will then eat the other seeds. Due to their higher fat content, from 10 to 20 per cent oats can be fed to birds kept outdoors in cold weather, birds in a moult, young budgies and breeding pairs with young in the nest.

All seeds should be viable and capable of germination to be valuable as food. Well cleaned, fresh seed from a reliable dealer can usually be depended upon for nutritional quality. Good quality canary seed and good quality millet are about equal in food value:

CANARY SEED: 14 per cent protein; 50 per cent carbohydrates; 5 per cent fat.

MILLET SEED: 12 per cent protein; 52 per cent carbohydrates; 4.5 per cent fat.

(The proteins of these seeds are deficient in essential amino-acids, notably lysine and arginine.)

Most breeders advocate the addition of cod-liver oil to the seed. Cod-liver oil contains toxic properties which can be detrimental to a budgie's health. The author and many of his breeder friends use a fine feeding oil instead, Diet-ol (trade name), which incorporates the principal values of wheat germ oil as well as fish-liver oil concentrates. Actually, dietary supplements adhering to the seed are almost entirely lost in the dehusking process.

SOAKED SEED

Soaking seeds is widely employed for breeding birds with young in the nest and for chicks when they leave the nest. Generally the method used is to immerse the seeds completely in water and to allow them to soak for 12 to 24 hours in order to soften them before feeding. This process actually drowns the seeds, leeches out valuable ingredients and encourages bacterial growth on the seeds.

The proper way to soak seeds is to invert a shallow pan inside of a wider pan, fill the outer, wider pan with water to within a half-inch of the rim. Then, on the top of the inverted pan lay a piece of coarse cloth or burlap, so that the edges of the cloth serve as wicks in keeping the whole cloth wet. Put the seeds on the cloth and they will keep moist without being drowned. The seed will begin to soften and swell, enzymic action will take place, changing and modifying the nutritional factors so that they are more readily absorbed and digested when eaten. A drop or two of feeding oil and a pinch of protein powder will add greatly to their nutritive value.

A new and inexpensive budgie seed, which incorporates medical specifics and antibiotics for the control of certain diseases, is now available to breeders. A standard amount of *chlortetracycline* is incorporated with hulled millet. The new seed, it is claimed, gives full protection against pneumonia, parrot fever, and other infectious diseases, as well as stimulating food intake and body growth. Similar foods have long been available to the breeders of commercial livestock and have drastically reduced mortality rates, controlled or eradicated some diseases and increased early market value through healthier, faster development. Budgie breeders are not interested in early market value, of course, but the other advantages of such a food should prove to be a boon to the fancy.

GREENS

Greens should be fed every day, or at least three times a week, in a quantity that can be consumed by the birds in about two hours. Dark green and leafy vegetation is best. Greens provide plant protein, minerals, vitamins, cellulose and water. In general, leafy vegetables are low in nutritional value since they are exceedingly

A great sky of imported breeding. A foundation sire, prepotent and virile, used successfully in back-crossing.

Australian Banded Pied Yellowface Cobalt (Type II). Good in size, color, spots. Band runs down to flank. Patchy in color on rump.

Australian Banded Pied Opaline Olive Green. Good color, markings, head and spots. Nice type. Band too large.

Australian Pied Opaline Blue (Type II). Nice, big bird of unusual color. Lacks frontal lift. Mask too small for spots.

Australian Pied Normal Cobalt. Very good size, type, color and color distribution. Band slightly small and patchy. Crouched stance due only to fright.

Australian Pied Normal Dark Green. Good markings but patchy in color, lacking in body and head size. Good spots but mask too small.

Australian Pied Opaline Skyblue. Big, nicely colored bird but appears somewhat long. Head lacking in skull. Missing spots, broken band.

bulky and contain so much water and cellulose. Cellulose is fiber and fiber is the skeleton of a plant, a non-soluble carbohydrate composed largely of hydrogen, oxygen and carbon, which has value only in prompting laxation. All commercially grown greens must be clean and fresh and should be carefully washed to remove toxic and poisonous sprays commonly used on plants to protect them from various infestations and diseases. Many greens, particularly wild-grown greens, as well as tree bark, have medicinal value.

A list of useful native grasses that can be gathered and fed during the spring and summer months and are easily available include: Alfalfa (a high protein and vitamin green) clover, chickweed, rye grass, dandelion, plantain, teazle and lawn clippings. Carrot, beet tops, corn raw or cooked and whatever fresh fruits your birds will eat can all be fed. Seeding grasses and greens are particularly relished by the birds.

The following plants must never be fed to birds as they produce phytotoxins (toxic substances) that cause poisoning: black locust, corn cockle, vetch seeds, cottonseed meal, crotalaria seed, daubentonia seeds, death camus, milkweed, nightshade, lily of the valley, and oleander.

Tree branches are heartily enjoyed by budgerigars, particularly the hens. They take great delight in stripping and consuming the fresh, green bark. Willow, apple, cherry (not sprayed), maple and various relatives of the eucalyptus can all supply branches and bark which budgies love, particularly the new branches in the spring that have leaf blossoms just opening.

When seasons change and fresh, growing greens are no longer available, their place can be taken by commercially grown greens such as celery (deep green varieties), broccoli, kale, spinach, carrot strips and tops, watercress, escarole, cabbage leaves and the many other vegetables sold for human consumption.

GRIT AND CUTTLEBONE

Grit acts as the teeth of the bird and is a necessity for bird digestion. There are several commercial grits which contain supplementary minerals and are good products. Charcoal, magnesium and limestone should not be used in grit fed to budgerigars. Two ingredients which should be included are ground granite and ground oystershell. A bare minimum of iodized salt can be included in the grit mix if it is not fed in any supplement provided for the birds.

Cuttlebone (or cuttlefish bone), plaster board, boiled egg shell and the commercially made calcium and mineral cubes are all good sources of the very necessary calcium and phosphorus. A piece of old mortar helps keep beaks trimmed and provides lime and other essentials.

Budgerigars enjoy chewing on all these substances. Oystershell is high in calcium carbonate and granite does not dissolve quickly and is, therefore, good grinding material. Milk is one of the best ways to feed calcium for it possesses a perfect balance of calcium and phosphorus. It is low in iron and copper but is a food rich in many other essentials, such as protein, fat and sugar, all in a form which is almost completely assimilated.

WATER

It is generally thought that budgerigars consume very little water. When constantly fed fresh greens this is fairly true since greens are so high in water content. But breeding birds and young birds consume a great deal of water and it should be supplied fresh and clean to all budgerigars at all times as an elementary nutritional essential. Water flushes the system, stimulates gastric juice activity, acts as a solvent within the body, and performs many other necessary and important jobs. It is a source of valuable minerals also and, being easily provided, it should be given freely.

VITAMINS AND MINERALS

Unlike several other species of animals, the budgerigar has not been fortunate enough to have been used as an experimental animal by investigators in nutrition. The result is that the dietary needs of some animals and birds have been established, but not the budgerigar's. Some little experimentation has been done and is being done, now that interest in better budgerigars is on the increase. Through this experimentation and the results in parallel fields of animal nutrition we know, as mentioned before, that our budgies need the three dietary essentials, proteins, carbohydrates and fats, in well balanced form. In addition to the big three all living creatures require an adequate intake of vitamins and minerals for bodily function. No minimum requirements for

Seafoam opaline showing the pastel factor, the blue factor, the opaline factor, and the third type of yellow-faced factor. This budgie also has one dark factor, giving it the cobalt blue shade.

A top winning normal sky of imported breeding, bred by Dominick Golia, Jr.

budgerigars have been established making it difficult to supply these factors in adequate and properly balanced potencies. If we are familiar with the various vitamins and minerals and their biologic functions, we can, however, decide which should be supplied in larger amounts than are recovered from natural foods. For instance, if we keep our birds indoors all year round, away from the sun, we will know that they are not getting enough vitamin D, therefore we must supply this vitamin in some synthetic form. If we find an eye anomaly in birds of long flight inheritance, it would seem wise to supply a supplementary high level of riboflavin (vitamin B_2 or G). Only in this manner can we overcome vitamin and mineral deficiency in our budgerigars when we have as yet no pertinent experimental data for reference.

The following table will supply the necessary fundamental sources and roles in nutrition of the various vitamins and minerals:—

VITAMINS

Vitamin	Biological Functions	Sources
Vitamin A	Growth, general metabolism. Prevention of infection. Prevention of one form of diarrhea. Fertility, reproduction, lactation and other glandular functions. Nerve and skin health, muscular co-ordination.	Egg yolk, butter, fish livers, carrots, milk, plant leaves and many dark green vegetables, alfalfa leaf meal.
Vitamin B (Complex)	Growth promotion, appetite, nerve and heart health, blood and liver function, fertility.	Yeast, cereals, milk, eggs, liver, fast growing plants, alfalfa leaf meal.
Biotin Pantothenic acid Riboflavin, thiamine Folic acid Niacin Pyridoxin	Gastrointestinal function and absorption. Lactation. Muscle function. Prevention of anemia, a specific type of paralysis.	Grains, seeds, grasses.
Vitamin C	Anti-scurvy vitamin.	Fruit juices, vegetables. Alfalfa, leaf meal.
Vitamin D (sunshine vitamin)	Utilization of calcium and phosphorus. Prevents rickets. Normal body structure and growth. Muscular co-ordination. Reproduction. Viability of young.	Fish livers and extracted oils. Some animal fats.

Vitamin E	Fertility. Growth. Survival. Pituitary gland health. Muscular development and co-ordination.	Seed germs. Wheat-germ oil. Vegetable oils.
Vitamin F	Blood clotting. Young bird health.	Alfalfa leaf meal. Specific feeding oils.
Unsaturated Fatty Acids (sometimes called Vit. F) Linoleic acid Linolenic acid Arachnidic acid	Feather and skin health.	Wheatgerm, linseed, and grapeseed oils. Many seed oils.

MINERALS

Mineral	Biological Functions	Sources
Calcium	Bone building. Muscle, nerve, heart function. Reproduction. Blood component.	Milk. Green ground bone-meal. Alfalfa leaf meal.
Phosphorus	Bone building. Carbohydrate and fat metabolism. Blood component. Liquid content of tissue.	Milk. Bone meal. Cereals. Meat. Fish.
Iron	Transports oxygen in blood. Components of red blood cells.	Egg yolk. Bone marrow. Liver, heart, gizzard.
Potassium and Sodium	Body fluid and blood regulator. Promotes normal growth and muscle function. Component of gastric juice and urine.	Blood. Table salt. Vegetables. Potatoes.
Magnesium	Normal growth and reproduction. Muscle activity. Nerve, blood.	Vegetables. Bonemeal.
Chloride	Blood, body fluid regulator. Component of gastric juices and urine.	Blood. Table salt.
Iodine	Thyroid health and normal growth. Regulates metabolism. Prevents goiter and cretinism.	Iodized salt. Oyster-shell. Plants from iron-rich soil.
Copper	Essential in formation of hemoglobin. Aids in growth of red blood cells and tissue respiration.	Blood. Copper sulfate.
Sulphur	Body regulation. Feather production.	Meat. Egg yolk. Protein rich foods.

NOTE.—*Manganese and zinc, two essential mineral trace elements, are needed in very minute amounts. Zinc is important to normal development of feathering.*

Cinamon green male, bred from show-winning English parents.

A pet Budgie with his toys. To alleviate this Opaline Green Budgie's loneliness, a plastic replica of a Budgie was supplied. The bird lavishes affection upon the dummy but wonders why his fondness is not returned.

This beautiful, show-winning hen from England is the dam of quality stock.

SUPPLEMENTARY FEEDING

Perhaps at this time a table of proteins, amino acids, their sources and properties should be listed. But the reader is perhaps weary by now of such tables so it will be omitted. Suffice it to say that proteins are found in animal meats, milk, cheese, eggs, animal organs, as the end product of digestion by gastric juice, feathers, hair, horny substances, blood and vegetable matter which produces vegetable proteins. Keratin, a protein which is found in high degree in feathers is also rich in sulphur, two important facts to remember.

We know now that budgerigars must be supplied with supplementary nutritional elements otherwise lacking in the basic diet, namely proteins and fats. They need these elements throughout their lives in order to keep healthy, fight disease, produce good feathering, be fertile and feed their young adequately. In Chapter 4 the physiologic process which takes place in the production of crop milk was explained. We know that crop milk is solidly protein and fats with vitamins and minerals associated with these essentials. It is true that budgies fed the basic diet alone, without supplementary feeding, produce generally adequate crop milk, but, in so doing, they are draining the crop milk substances from their own body tissues which have labored hard to extract and synthesize proteins and fats from the meagre allowance in their basic diet. Animal protein as well as plant protein must be fed to budgerigars, for animal protein contains different, essential amino acids of high value. Fed the basic diet only, the budgerigar must convert inferior protein of low biologic value by means of its crop bacteria into protein superior enough to give growth and nutrition to its young. This is an exceedingly difficult undertaking.

Experiments in growth rates, employing both the cafeteria (self choice) and breeder's choice techniques in feeding the breeding budgerigar with young in nest, show beyond a doubt that they need high-protein supplementary feeding. These tests establish several interesting facts.

There is competition within the individual chick between body growth and feather growth and both depend upon proteins for development.

The ability to feed their progeny well over several nests is

Pet Budgerigars make a beautiful display in the home.

apparently an inherited character in parent birds. Some pairs could produce and feed well feathered, well grown, vigorous young for as many as five to seven consecutive nests on protein supplementary diets. Other control parent pairs from similar breeding as the birds above, but fed only the basic diet without supplements, produced small, brittle-feathered weaklings in the third nest, and thereafter broke their fertile eggs before they hatched. Other parent pairs on the supplementary diet produced three nests of large, vigorous chicks but weaklings in the fourth nest. The same parent birds in a previous season were not fed a supplementary diet and produced a percentage of French moult in the first two nests.

In normally grown chicks the critical nutritional period arrives immediately after they have been removed from the parents to the nursery flight. Growth curves show a decided drop or leveling off at this time since the chicks are in a period of increased activity and feather growth is coupled with a lack of ability to achieve adequate food intake.

Chicks in nest boxes deliberately exposed to heavy mite infestation showed no great difference in growth curves and did not necessarily display French moult.

Some parent pairs can have many more nests of vigorous young and care for and adequately nourish more young in individual nests than do others. But, better general growth in the progeny is obtained when parent pairs are limited to the rearing of three or four young in each nest.

A budgerigar chick, in the first twenty days of its life will show a weight increase of from twenty to twenty-five times its hatching weight—a truly dramatic growth.

Supplementary food must show a high level of proteins, lecithin, and vitamin A (crop-milk is rich in these substances), riboflavin and the B vitamins for hatchability, a fairly high level of fatty acids, niacin, phosphorus, calcium, sodium, manganese and other minerals and vitamins. Keratin should be one of the proteins definitely supplied. The necessary nutrients should be balanced, the texture of the supplement must be correct, and it must be highly palatable. The protein requirement for best nutrition is dependent upon the quality of the protein amino acid composition and their interaction. It is best to feed combined animal and plant protein to insure balanced amino acid intake, for proteins (excepting milk which contains all essential amino acids) have unequal properties, according to their source. Protein rich foods which can be used in the supplementary diet are milk, dehydrated eggs, boiled fresh eggs, raw and cooked ground meats, alfalfa leaf meal, soybean meal, cheese, fish meals, and liver meal.

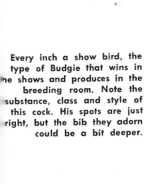

Every inch a show bird, the type of Budgie that wins in the shows and produces in the breeding room. Note the substance, class and style of this cock. His spots are just right, but the bib they adorn could be a bit deeper.

In zoos, where valuable birds are kept, supplementary diets are fed to all birds of the parrot family. In general, these supplements contain about 50 per cent ground grains, such as whole wheat, whole barley, rolled oats, yellow corn, and 35 per cent foods high in protein value, such as peanut meal, alfalfa leaf meal, soybean meal, dried milk, and dehydrated eggs. Added are brewer's yeast, oyster-shell flour, about two per cent of a good A and D vitamin feeding oil and one per cent iodized salt. Nine parts of this mixture is blended with one part of ground boiled meat and its broth to make a mash. A substitute diet used in zoos which closely dupli-

Cinnamon green and cinnamon sky brothers. These young birds are bred to produce.

Imported green of tremendous substance. This bird has produced several top show winners.

cates the above diet is prepared by mixing 78 per cent of a good dog-meal, ten per cent ground cooked meat, ten per cent freshly grated raw carrots, and two per cent feeding oil.

The author mixes a supplementary diet consisting of hard-boiled eggs, brown rice boiled in salted vegetable juices, cooked or raw hamburger, infants' applesauce, grated raw carrots, whole or evaporated milk and various left-over mashed vegetables, such as peas, beans, and broccoli. The result is a fairly wet mixture to which is added, dry dog-meal or chicken egg mash, for proper consistency, feeding oil, which contains vitamins A, D, E and F, and a small amount of Aurovim, a product for growth stimulation, which contains Aureomycin, vitamins B_{12}, A and D, and niacin, riboflavin and pantothenate. When birds are breeding and young are in the nest a small amount of melted butter is added to the diet. The mixture, when properly prepared, has a crumbly texture and high palatability. The breeding birds and young chicks in particular consume it in large quantities, seed consumption falling off drastically in preference to the supplement. A cup of a dry mixture of dog-meal and egg food or ground wheat, oats, and corn (chick scratch) is also available in each cage and flight.

Food and water should be constantly available to the birds not fed at specific times, for budgerigars like to nibble and eat frequently during the day. Their heaviest intake of food is in the morning, and at night just before dark.

Feeding ranks next to breeding in the influence it exerts upon the stock. Knowledgeable breeding can produce genetically fine specimens, selection can improve the strain but, without full and proper nourishment, particularly during the period of growth, superior budgerigars will not be obtained. The slogan of a cattle breeder might well be adopted by breeders of better budgerigars: "Breed, feed, weed."

MANAGEMENT

Whatever pleasure one gets out of life must be paid for in some kind of coin. With our budgerigars we must pay the toll of constant care for they are completely dependent on us.

Good husbandry pays off in dollars and cents as well as in satisfaction. Clean, well-cared-for budgerigars are most often healthy budgerigars, free from parasitic invaders and the small ills

A top winning green cock with an almost owlish look!

Cinnamon green male. A big bird with good substance, bred to produce.

Both these birds are good in type, but when one examines them closely it becomes evident that the bird on the right is a much better exhibition specimen. This Budgie is larger, shows a better brow, has a greater aura of breeding worth, and sports a fine set of spots. White bib feathers shroud the shape of the spots and should be plucked out. These are both German birds.

that bring other and greater woes in their wake. Proper feeding and facilities for adequate exercise help build strength and resistance to disease. So, through good husbandry and management, veterinarian bills and nursing time are substantially reduced, saving money and time, and often saving that particularly outstanding youngster which will put the enthusiast on the road to breeding and exhibition success.

Cleanliness is the first essential of good management. The floors of the bird room should be vacuumed at least twice a week, particularly during times of heavy moult. The many and varied attachments which accompany most vacuums are useful in cleaning flights and even smaller cages. Unconsumed green food should be removed daily and paper laid on the floor of flights. This can be easily bundled up and removed.

As mentioned before, a paint scraper will be found to be a handy tool to scrape metal trays free of accumulated droppings. Once a week at least, all food pans and dishes for water and food, as well as water troughs and tubes, should be washed in hot water containing either soap, soda, or detergent, and rinsed thoroughly. Once a week, spray all the birds with a good parasitic specific, a liquid made especially for birds which contains no toxic ingredients. About once a month, scrape accumulated debris from the perches.

During the breeding season, daily inspection of the nest boxes is in order. Check to see if the young are being fed properly, that hens are not egg-bound, that the nest boxes are not wet or require cleaning, and that hens are not feather-plucking their young. Don't disturb the hen by too much cleaning. Instead, replace the sawdust or other material used with a fresh supply. If no nesting material is used and the nest is wet and bacterial growth is beginning, replace the block with a clean one. The less the nest box is disturbed the better. As soon as the young have left the nest box, remove the block, spray inside with a disinfectant, and put in a fresh block.

Seeds should be kept in metal containers with tightly fitting tops so that they are vermin-proof. They should be kept in a dry place; dampness will cause mold and rot. Check seed pots and hoppers to be sure that there is always a constant supply of seeds readily available.

After the breeding season is completed the annual cleaning should take place. Netting should be inspected, necessary painting should be done, and breeding cages and nest boxes thoroughly cleaned, disinfected, and stored away.

Twice a year, all birds should be wormed by using a derivative of one of the new and harmless, yet effective, drugs on the market. These can be added to the food without any trouble. Birds, like most animals, are subject to internal and external parasitic infestation. The symptoms—ruffled, puffed up appearance, soiled vent—are familiar to most breeders. Sick birds should be isolated immediately. Care should always be taken in catching birds so that they are not injured in the process. A net made especially for this purpose should be employed.

Birds should be placed in new quarters early in the day so they will become accustomed to new surroundings by nightfall. Once settled down for the night they should not be disturbed or startled.

The secret of good management is never to keep more stock than can be easily cared for; otherwise the work involved becomes a disagreeable job instead of an interesting and pleasurable occupation.

Good feeding and management are the most important part of budgerigar health and disease prevention. Without them you cannot expect to produce better budgerigars. The future of your stock is in your hands; a small amount of labor daily is your budgerigars' health and life insurance.

A quartet   of Budgies illustrating various color
phases. At the far left is a Normal Sky and
next to the blue are three birds that fall into
the Green category, indicating the change
in color shade when the Gray factor is added
and when the sex-linked Cinnamon factor
effects the basic color.

Chapter 7
SELECTION AND UPGRADING

The most engrossing and eagerly awaited time for the earnest breeder is when the young from a particularly important mating, have reached an age when they can be initially assessed for quality. The chicks in any given nest will, of course, vary in quality and, therefore, the novice can only select by limited comparison. But the breeder who has had previous experience with quality stock and handled many nests of young is not limited in selection by a single-nest comparison. He has retained a mental picture of the early appearance of outstanding young in the nests he has bred before. To the novice, a few breeders seem to possess an uncanny skill in selecting the best from a nest of fledgelings not yet old enough to leave the nest box. This facility is neither luck nor sorcery, it is simply applying experience to the knowledge of what to look for in a baby budgerigar.

SELECTION IN THE NEST

When the poults have become clothed in their first coat of feathers, but before the feathering has reached full completion, remove each chick from the nest box separately and hold it with full-face facing you. From the feel of its body bulk in your hand you will be able to gauge substance and body size in relation to other chicks you have handled. Next examine the feet and legs which will indicate by their size the eventual size at maturity of the chick. A big, heavy-footed baby will develop into a big bird that will balance when adult, the size of its underpinning. Then, and most important, examine the head as seen from the front. Look for heaviness, great width between the eyes and "browiness," a slight jutting of the skull immediately above the eyes. This accentuation of the brow, coupled with skull width, is particularly important in female chicks.

A trio of Pied Budgerigars. The bird in the center is an Opaline. Note the frontal flecks on the mature bird at the left. This is a fault ("Dirty head") difficult to breed out.

Cinnamon green cock from a famous English cinnamon line.

A winning green pied of the dominant Dutch variety.

Check the band numbers of those chicks which you select in the nest by this method and you will generally find that they mature into the best birds. There are, of course, many other aspects of type and quality which must be considered in an exhibition budgerigar but which cannot be evaluated at this age. Generally you will find that big fledgelings with large, heavy feet and big, wide and round heads, develop into quality stock. A famous cattle judge once said, "Show me the front end of an animal, head on, and I'll tell you what's behind the head and feet!" This sage remark holds true for budgerigars too, since conformation, skeletal balance and overall structural rhythm usually conform closely to the modeling of the face and head.

LEAVING THE NEST

After the young quit the nest they should be allowed to remain in the breeding compartment for a week or 10 days longer. During this time, while the hen begins another clutch of eggs, it becomes the sire's duty to feed his young. At this point each youngster should be equipped with a family band of specific color or colors. Later, when old enough to be put into the larger flight with many other birds of different parentage, a glance at this leg band, without catching or handling the bird, can quickly divulge the bird's breeding.

At first the youngsters will keep popping in and out of the nest box, often to the hen's discomfort and even anger, if she has new eggs in the nest. But, after a few days they will remain out, taking to the perches. Most chicks learn how to shell and eat the kernal of seeds while still in the nest box, since seeds are often brought to them and deposited on the bottom of the nest box by the parent birds. Once out of the nest box, they will quickly learn how to eat if they have not been taught before, and seed and supplement must be readily available to them on the floor of the breeding cage. Seed can be scattered on the floor or confined to shallow containers such as you will use for the supplement. Jar tops can be utilized for this purpose. Soaked seed, fortified with a high protein and vitamin powder, can also be supplied at this time.

There is a sudden and definite lapse of growth rate in the young once they leave the nest if they do not have the benefit of auxiliary feeding by the parent cock, since they are not able by themselves to consume enough food to permit steady growth during this period. Occasionally a male will not feed his chicks once they leave the nest, or the babies are knocked off the perches, are pecked at and generally harassed by either or both parents. When this occurs, the chicks should be removed from the breeding cage and put in the nursery flight cage. If the chicks have made free of the nest box during the laying of the next clutch and have fouled the new eggs, it is a good idea, once they have been removed, to clean the eggs of accumulated filth. Do not try to scrape the dirt off with your finger nail, even when it has been soaked. Gently soak the eggs in warm water, separately, until most of the accumulated dirt has soaked off, then dry them with a towel. Handle with care, please, for these tiny eggs are very delicate and easily broken.

THE NURSERY FLIGHT

The size of the nursery flight is dependent upon the number of youngsters it must accommodate, yet it should never be too large. A length of three to four feet with depth and height approaching two feet is about as large as the nursery cage should be, since the chicks must here learn to use their wings and thus never be too far from the food and water supply. Food, grit, cuttlebone or substitute, water and supplement should be abundant and constantly available in shallow, easily accessible pans.

At each end of this flight a show cage should be attached, the side resting against the nursery flight open to conform to an equal opening in the flight cage wire. The floor of these show cages should be covered with seed and they should also contain some tidbit to which the youngsters are particularly partial, such as spray millet or clover. The inquisitive chicks will soon discover the extra cages and their contents, the slower ones will eventually follow and will always thereafter associate the show cage with something pleasant. In this manner you effortlessly begin the show training of young stock.

Many breeders use an old, peaceful male in the nursery flight to act as bell-mare for the youngsters, guiding them to food and water. After about four to six weeks in the nursery flight, the youngsters can be removed to a larger flight. If youth flights are

One of the first olive greens, a color variety in which the basic green is effected by two dark factors. This cock also displays the opaline pattern, a sex-linked mutation.

A young, well bred lutino, the red-eye, albino phase of the green series.

not separately maintained where they can be kept until after their first moult, they can be put immediately into the large flights with the adult birds. Before they are transferred from the nursery flight, all the young should be sexed and the sexes kept separately from then on.

A nice Opaline Blue of good type and stance, showing normal wing pattern. Note the large head and the solidity of the well modeled skull. Exhibited in Germany this cock deservedly topped some excellent competition in that country. Mask should be cleared of extra spotting.

SEXING THE YOUNG

The cere of the budgerigar is most frequently consulted to determine the sex of the young bird. In females, even in the nest, it is less prominent, not as fully lobed, flatter and less pink than in the males. Cock fledgelings, out of the nest, usually exhibit such an intense pinkness of the cere that it actually has an appearance of soreness. In hens, white and pale blue, almost approaching the color of mother-of-pearl, begins to make its appearance on the cere. Hens, when handled, will generally make more of a fuss and bite harder and with greater tenaciousness than cock birds. When startled, the young hen's cere will show a paler rim immediately circling the nostrils.

To the experienced breeder secondary sex characteristics are even more dependable. Head shape, stance, color, behavior and even the shape of the pelvic girdle when felt through the feathering, all play their part in sex determination. As the chicks become older, the cere of the male will gradually turn to a deep blue, while that of the hen becomes whiter with pale blue tinting and, eventually, becomes tan, then brown.

Sex determination by cere study is difficult in some of the red-eyed varieties and recessive pieds, and the best indication is through cere shape and the secondary characteristics.

In strains, established by line or inbreeding, the breeder, familiar with his stock, has less difficulty in sexing the young, since he has learned, over several generations, the differentiating sexual characteristics peculiar to his strain.

CULLING OF YOUNG

From selection in the nest you can be fairly certain which of the youngsters you will retain for future breeding or showing. But to be completely sure wait until after the first moult is finished. This takes place when the fledgelings are approximately four months of age. The time to cull and select has arrived. Once this moult is completed and the young are resplendent in their new, vari-colored cloaks, their sex visibly established, they will exhibit the promise they will achieve at full maturity.

Culling should begin at the bottom. Select your poorest young-sters and separate them. These you will dispose of. Then compare the birds which you have left with each other, divided by sex and variety. Remember there is and should be a difference in type between the sexes, mostly noticeable in the head. This should be "selected for" and preserved. You will perhaps find a few more to put in the "out" cage. Those which are left should be put in show cages separately or in twos, and evaluated. Grade them as recommended in Chapter 3 (see Linebreeding). Any bird ex-hibiting two or more major faults and given less than a G+ rating should be discarded. The youngsters rated E− to E+ should be good enough for exhibition. Those receiving a rating of G+ should be retained exclusively for specific breedings.

A huge sky cock of Scotch breeding, always at the top when shown, and a producer of quality stock.

The greywing factor is a "dilute" factor. All colors are intermediate between the pale and dark factors. This was one of the early "rate" factors. Comparison of this early greywing with good dilutes of today is an indication of the progress that can be made by knowledgable breeders in any variety.

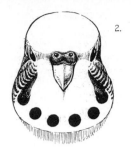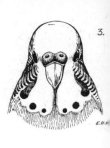

1. Excellent cock head. 2. Excellent hen head. 3. Faulty head—narrow, pinched too sma
Spots small and uneven in size. Cheeks flat. Bifurcated and scalloped mask.

Next examine the pedigrees of the choice young to ascertain which of your parent birds have produced the greatest number of quality young, which the second greatest amount, and so on. Check these findings against the number of young produced by each mating and so reach a percentage ratio. In this manner it can be determined which genetic combinations are producing the best and most promising chicks.

Lastly, compare the young with their parents, segregated by sex. If the young of any given breeding are not up to the quality of their parents, then the mating cannot be considered successful. The parent pair should be disposed of or broken up for recombination with other mates which might prove more suitable.

1. Excellent cock head (profile) 2. Excellent hen head (profile).

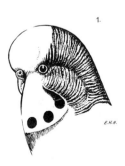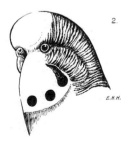

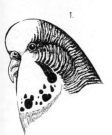

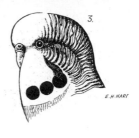

FAULTY HEADS: 1. Pinhead: topskull (crown) falls away abruptly and backskull is completely missing. Protruding upper mandible. Eye set too high and too close to nasal parts. Multiple throat spots. 2. Lack of frontal. Beak too long. Mask too short. Throat spots too small and flat-topped. 3. Flattened topskull (crown). Nipped in neck. Spots too large for bib width.

The youngsters from such breedings should not be used for breeding. Only chicks which show improvement over the parent stock, or in the case of top quality breeding birds, are of equal quality, should be kept for future breeding. If the young from any particular pair fall below the G+ classification generally, with only an occasional top quality youngster hatched, then the parents should be discarded. The occasional good youngster should be kept and experimentally bred to determine whether the particular excellent youngster possesses that happy genetic combination from parental forebears which will enable it to produce quality progeny. Until the chick's genetic possibilities have been ascertained, it should not be used in strain breeding. But, should the genetic background of the pair which produces only an occasional quality chick, be not completely satisfactory, then even the better-than-average youngsters should be disposed of so that there will be no temptation to use them for breeding which would downgrade your stock.

While grading the youngsters, pay strict attention to the standard, employing it as a yardstick of comparison. Initially examine the birds from a distance to assess size, shape and balance which, combined with condition, accounts for 30 points in the exhibition scale. Then, move closer to examine the finer points of the bird. The *Budgerigar Fault Finder*, which cleverly shows the many faults budgerigars are heir to, can be of great assistance at this time.

A group of pet Budgies, colorful and charming.

A fine young white (pastel) of English and Scotch breeding. This color is the result of a double recessive.

In the standard scale only 15 points are allotted to mask and spots and 20 to size and shape of head, giving us but 35 points for these anatomic sections out of a possible 100 point total. Even if a bird displayed rare quality in all the virtues covered by the other 65 points he would still not stand a chance on the show bench, unless he excelled in head, mask and spots. Of course, quality in these sections alone does not make a top show bird and, for the breeder, therefore, overall quality is essential for progress.

In the pastel, clearwing and albino series no points are allotted for mask and spots. Yet, in selecting your own stock, depth of bib and size and spacing of spots (in pastel and clearwing) should be sought for, since lack of quality in one section will eventually lead to lack in another. In the opaline variety, five points are added to color on the scale, which can be interpreted as meaning distribution and intensity. In wing series birds, clearwing, greywing (dilute) and cinnamon, 10 points are added to wing markings.

Some faults can be utilized and made into assets instead of liabilities in the breeding cage. Birds possessing double rows of spots or spots so huge that they overlap, can produce large, well placed spots when bred to mates with medium or small but evenly spaced spots, if bibs, wide and deep enough to support the larger spots, can also be bred. Drop-winged birds can, in the breeding cage, be used as a counterweight to birds which carry their wings too high.

UPGRADING

To upgrade your stock you must cull ruthlessly and retain only the best producers and, of course, develop a system of line or inbreeding which will produce high family quality. Each season's breedings should bring an ever increasing ratio of excellent young. Your records will indicate which pairs and which families are giving you this higher grade quality. Even these basic, able birds should be discarded if their progeny produce, on the average, better budgerigars. Keep the younger and better producers. The appearance of a bird, no matter how outstanding, must not sway the breeder. His worth, in upgrading, can only be measured by his success as a stud.

A definite rise in type and wanted virtues should continue year after year. The extent of this rise in quality can be ascertained by comparing your top birds of today with those of a few seasons back. Family lines which do not give you this improvement should be eliminated from your breeding plans. This steady climb in overall quality should be so definitely apparent that, in comparison, budgerigars which you rated E two or three seasons before would now be graded only G. Thus, only by strict selection and ruthless elimination can you upgrade your stock and progress toward the establishment of ever greater quality in your aviary.

ESTABLISHING A STRAIN

A strain is a family within a breed which possesses definite and individual characteristics which consistently breed true.

After several breeding seasons, you will know which of your parent pairs are producing, on the average, the best progeny. In Chapter 3 (see Linebreeding), you found a list of recommended rules to follow for the establishment of a strain. Apply these rules to the chicks from your best producing pairs. From the selected few which were graded highly and exhibit early fertility, by cere color and actions, you will set up your next season's breedings. Do not use any bird no matter how excellent in quality, who has been a poor doer or has had French moult and recovered.

To start a strain you must first inbreed. If you have produced an outstanding cock from a quality dam in this season's breeding, breed him back to his mother. If it should be a hen from a top quality sire, breed her back to her father. Of the young from this breeding, select those which most closely mirror the type and quality of their excellent parent. Meanwhile you will select a brother or sister of the outstanding bird which was originally bred back to its parent and breed this quality brother or sister to a top bird produced by one of your other pairs which display high quality in any characteristic lacking in the initial brecding. Choose from the progeny those which most closely resemble the quality parent once again, and any young which display wanted improvement needed in any structural phase. These and similar breedings should be carried out with as many pairs as possible. Mathematically, the more pairs you breed, the greater number of young exhibiting varied genetic combinations you will have for selection.

To clarify the breeding combinations employed to found a line, we will fashion a mythical pedigree using as symbols, **X** (sire)

The bird at the left is of nice general type and sits well on the perch. The spots are nicely spaced and of a good size for the bib though, for an exhibition bird, we generally prefer to see the spots larger.

This bird is drooping its tail, a fault usually of the moment though not always. Frequently the bird becomes frightened when it is photographed and drops its tail in this manner. Both these birds are of German origin.

ow Face Opaline Mauve. d size and color. Bad ce, head too small, multiple spots.

Opaline Grey Green. Good color, size and markings. Fairly good spots. Lacks frontal rise. In momentarily bad stance.

Opaline Olive Green. Good size, type and color, though the latter somewhat patchy. Good hen's head, nipped in neck.

rmal Light Green. Good e throughout. Good d. Color slightly chy. Spots irregular. Mask could be deeper.

Normal Dark Green Cock. Excellent in type and stance. Good head. Color slightly patchy. Mask and spots slightly uneven.

Yellow Face Skyblue (Type II). Very good even color and markings. Too small throughout. Lacks frontal rise. Spots too small.

and **O** (dam) for the original parent pair and **Y** (sire) and **Z** (dam) for the outcross parent pair.

LINEBRED PROGENY
(Strain)

$$
\text{X OO} \begin{cases} \text{X O} \begin{cases} \text{X} \\ \text{O} \star \end{cases} \\ \text{O} \star \end{cases}
$$

$$
\text{XOYZ} \begin{cases} \text{Y Z} \begin{cases} \text{Y} \\ \text{Z} \end{cases} \\ \text{X O} \begin{cases} \text{X} \\ \text{O} \star \end{cases} \end{cases}
$$

With this breeding you now have stock which is based strongly on your best pair of birds with particular emphasis upon the genetic quality of your finest bird the **O** hen. The one outcross, **Y-Z,** brought in needed improvement. If this improvement could be found in birds related to the **X-O** pair in any degree, it would make an even better breeding to introduce. The pedigree makes it obvious that inbreeding and linebreeding reduces the relative number of ancestors and in the strain stresses the best genetic material available in the stud.

---

 * In upgrading and establishing strains with rares of the recessive types (autosomal mutations) a different approach must be made. In most instances mutation brings with it regression to the wild type, obvious by smaller size, spots, heads, etc. Quick improvement toward better quality, even with dominant rares (dominant pied, etc.) can be made by breeding two unrelated rares to two closely inbred, quality normals. The resulting splits (in the case of recessive rares) should then be bred together and the approximately 25 per cent rares recovered should exhibit vast improvement. The quality, inbred normal birds employed, should possess such prepotency that they will stamp the progeny, to a large degree, with their own type and quality.

The beginning of a strain has now been established. To continue the strain you must consistently breed back within the family you have established. Good matings for this purpose are, half-brother to half-sister, grandfather to granddaughter, uncle to niece, father to daughter. Remember that selection, particularly for those family qualities which stamp the strain with individuality, must always be adhered to.

After your strain has become established, it is possible that you may find it lacking to some degree in one or more desired qualities. Let us assume that your strain fails in spots. To correct this failure the breeder is often tempted to introduce immediately an outcross of large-spotted stock. But to do so would bring in other unwanted characteristics which the breeder has all but eliminated in his strain. It will also result in a lack of uniformity in the progeny and loss of the control of genetic combinations which the breeder has established. Instead of bringing in the raw outcross to breed directly into his strain, the breeder should begin a new strain with the well spotted outcross using mates from his established strain. Selection from the resultant progeny should include the desired features, large spots, as well as the features already established in the basic strain. The progeny should then be line or inbred, in much the same manner in which the original strain was established with constant selection for the needed improvement. Finally, when the improvement has been "fixed" in the second strain, the two strains are fused to produce the wanted improvement, without the loss of strain identity.

It is always wise to develop two or more strains originally based on relationships but each strain, in its own right, excelling in some specific quality or qualities. These strains can, when necessary, be blended to achieve improvement without the loss of those characteristics which mark your strain.

At the end of the breeding season, check results against previous seasons. Some families may show decline in fertility and you will know then that in selecting for type, size and other visible qualities, you have neglected this most important characteristic in an inbred or linebred strain. New and vigorous genetic material must then be brought into the strain. This can be done by crossing to one of the other lines bred from related ancestry which exhibit no fertility decline.

Opaline Cinnamon Skyblue. Good color and markings, good head and deportment. Color somewhat patchy, multiple spots.

Opaline Cobalt. Good size, color and markings. Excellent spots. Lacks frontal rise. Bad stance due to fright.

Skyblue. Good size, c and markings. Nippe neck. Irregular sp Hangs over pe

Normal Mauve. Patchy color, no spots. Head small, lacks frontal rise. Tail faulty. Not in show condition.

Normal Grey. (Light phase). Good color and markings. Faulty stance, drooping tail, flat head, irregular spots.

Normal Violet. Fine co good type, markings stance. Lacks in top sk depth of mask and siz sp

A young Lutino which is the albino phase in the Green series. Richness of color is very desirable along with complete lack of any green suffusion. This color variety is sex-linked. The depth of rich yellow combined with the albinistic red eye makes this an attractive variety that has found great favor with the fancy.

A breeder can be justly proud of a strain of quality stock which is the result of his own breeding skill and so individual in type that other, knowledgeable fanciers can tell at a glance that these particular budgerigars originated, or come from the strain which the breeder has established. The size of a stud or aviary, the amount of money spent in birds or equipment, the number and quality of birds bought, shown, and won with, are no substitutes, in themselves, for breeding skill and knowledge.

BODY FAULTS OF BUDGERIGARS

1. Short-sided; not enough length in body. High wing carriage. Lump on withers. Opaline saddle is not clear.

2. Hollow in back. Rump raised. Dropped tail. Pronounced stomach.

3. Crossed wings. Lack of substance. Heart-shaped spots.

Greywing Olive Green. Very good color and markings. Lacking badly in frontal rise. Shows long flight characteristics.

Normal Yellow. Very good type and size. Color appears almost olive. Markings too dark for Buttercup.

Olive Green. Good type and color, but m ings faulty through namon influence. not even in

Greywing Cobalt. Satisfactory color and markings but extremely long-flighted, hence bad stance. Head too flat and small. Spots too small.

Yellow Face Greywing Skyblue (Type I). Good color and stance. Markings excellent. Excellent condition. Tail drooped.

Normal Greywing Sk Good color and st Markings too light. in skull size, fronta and shows slightly br mask, no s

A wild Budgie, normal light green, racy in type and capable of existing in the wild state.

4. Hoopy carriage. Lying over perch.
Dropped wings.

In England and Scotland some of the most successful breeders and exhibitors have been Watmough, Kirby-Mason and Dabner, Rothery, Finey, Collyer, Farmer, Wait, North, Landsburg, Bryan, Miller, Fulgoni, and McCleary. The top studs in this country have generally been based on the bloodlines of the aforementioned English and Scotch breeders, particularly Bryan, North, Fulgoni, Miller and McCleary.

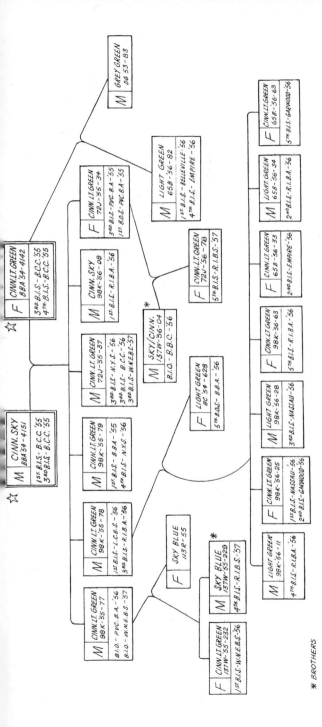

True chart illustrating breeding the potency of an imported winning pair of related Budgerigars. Note how this quality, through judicious matings, is passed on to proceeding generations. Only major wins are listed. Open class wins were made in shows where B.I.O. was not permitted to compete for B. I. S.

Key:—
M=Male   B.I.S. = Best in Show (and place number)
F=Female   B.O.S. = Best Opposite Sex (and place number)
B.I.O. = Best in Open Class
Initials after win listings indicate shows where wins were made.

* BROTHERS

173

Because of the many mutations in color and pattern, the Budgie is one of the most variegated and beautiful of birds. Breeders, quick to recognize new phases, have increased the Budgie's optical fascination by selecting for and breeding them in a rainbow array of brilliant colors. Above are examples of the basic Green Budgie (on the left), a Cobalt Normal, a Grey Normal, and an Opaline Light Green.

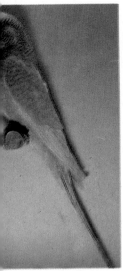  

Wing Light Green.
good type and
. Markings too
on neck and part of
wings.

Yellow Wing Dark Green.
Excellent color and good
contrast in wings and
body color. Lacks type,
stance and head qualities.

Normal Cinnamon Grey-green. Excellent color and
markings, excellent type.
Dropped tail due to fright
Spots irregular.

ewing Skyblue. Good
color, markings,
Needs frontal rise.
y stance (resting
body on perch).

Whitewing Cobalt. Excellent color. White wings
satisfactory. Good type
though head could be
larger.

Normal Cinnamon Violet.
Good markings and fair
color due to patchiness.
Head too small. Stance
not correct.

Chapter 8
TROUBLE HINTS AND AILMENTS

The budgerigar, when properly fed and cared for, is normally a healthy bird. Yet, as are all living creatures, the budgerigar is heir to many illnesses, some specific, some infectious and some parasitic. Among the nonspecific diseases are those caused by nutritional imbalance, deficient diets, impaired assimilation of food (metabolic), toxic intake and poisons. The symptoms of illness in the budgerigar are generally obvious and the puffed, huddled sick appearance is recognized by all.

If you are fortunate enough to have a veterinarian near who takes an interest in budgerigar diseases and treatment, your wisest course is to take your sick bird to him immediately upon recognition of signs of illness, particularly if the budgie is of value as a breeder or exhibition bird. The author does not feel qualified to give advice about treatment for the many ills which can beset our birds. By the same token, the reader is seldom qualified to treat those ills with the skill or knowledge necessary for success. Therefore, this chapter is merely a resume of modern findings on the most prevalent illnesses, so that you can either recognize the symptoms, eliminate the causative agent if possible or, in case of a noncommunicable disease, experiment in the art of healing.

The effect and appearance of the budgerigar in the majority of the diseases which beset him are so similar that it is difficult to diagnose them specifically. The sick bird may display any of the following symptoms: Loss of appetite, watery, discolored feces, the typical ruffling of feathers and squinting of eyes, head tucked under wing, discharge from eyes or nostrils, convulsions, sometimes excessive thirst and general debility. When these signs appear, either alone or in combination, remove the ill bird immediately to isolated quarters in a hospital cage kept at a temperature of 85°F. The birds which have been exposed should be watched carefully for any signs of illness. If you do not have a hospital cage, use any small cage. Drape three sides of the cage with cloth and place a small, lit electric lamp against the fourth side of the cage. A thermometer hung on the cage will aid in keeping the temperature even and at the proper heat. Heat is definitely the first essential in the treatment of sick birds. If the bird is eating, a little sugar or honey mixed with the food will aid in recovery. If you administer liquid medication of any kind with a medicine dropper, be very careful to give but one drop at a time, otherwise you might choke the bird.

PARASITES (Internal)

Coccidiosis is caused by a single-celled protozoa and generally affects birds which are allowed the freedom of outdoor flights since it is usually passed on to them by wild birds which land on the roof or side wire of the flights. Loose and bloody stools, weakness, loss of appetite, are indicative of the presence of this disease. In birds this disease is quite easily cured by the adminis-tration of one of the various sulfa drugs.

Roundworms, flukes, tapeworms and other internal parasites can be detected by the appearance of their eggs in the bird's droppings. Through microscopic examination your veterinarian can diagnose and prescribe specific medication for the eradication of these parasites. The new, nontoxic, easily used worm eradicator, Piperazine, is an excellent worm expellent for birds.

PARASITES (External)

Mouth canker, sometimes confused with scaley face, is caused by a single-celled organism and can be eradicated by a series of applications of any medication that will kill parasites and heal without harming the bird.

Mites of many kinds, and feather lice are the plague of the breeder, though these vicious little arachnids can be easily controlled. A three per cent pyrethrum powder, often available in dog and cat flea powders, should be dusted under the wings and around the vent. Be sure the powder you use does not contain DDT, derris root or rotenone. There are several excellent Freon sprays, commercially packaged for mite eradication, which are also excellent. The use of a good spray, combined with the dusting, will eliminate these tiny feather and skin chewers and blood suckers from the birds.

A young Normal Budgerigar. Note the striations covering the skull to the cere, also the looped markings on the mask, both indicative of the fact that the bird has not yet gone through its three months moult. After the moult the barring on the forehead will have disappeared and the indecisive markings on the mask will have become necklace spots.

Above are shown two birds displaying the newest mutational adornment, the crest. Both birds are mature cocks, and both are Green. The bird on the left is a Graywing Light Green; the other is a Normal Dark Green. The crest can be bred in three basic forms and with several variations within the three forms.

The next step is to eliminate these minute monsters from your flights and cages. Scrubbing with hot water, yellow soap, and a good disinfectant will help. Perch paint, designed for mite elimination, can be applied to the perches and corners of flights and cages. Change the cuttlebones or mineral blocks and disinfect any food holders, all cracks, edges and perch ends.

Scaley leg is also caused by a mite which infests the leg scales and sometimes the skin of the face around the beak and cere. Aureomycin salve, sulphur-base skin lotion or any of the trade-name products, such as Sca-Fade or Scalex, are all effective medication.

A fungus can also cause a species of what is termed scaley face. This can be cured by the application of any of the above products, a good fungicide, or the new antibiotic, Malucidin.

DIARRHEA

Diarrhea is usually a symptom of disease rather than a disease in itself. It can cause serious dehydration because the budgerigar possesses such a small reserve supply of water. Simple diarrhea can be caused by laxative foods and can be cured by withholding all greens and fruits and by administering milk of bismuth or Kaopectate. These liquids can be applied to the seed or added to an egg, hard boiled and mashed, which can be fed as a supplement. Strong tea or boiled milk can be given instead of water. If non-infectious diarrhea is caused by abnormal intestinal bacteria from bad foods, an antibiotic in the drinking water will bring quick relief.

SPECIFIC DISEASES

This group has a single cause as opposed to nonspecific diseases which are caused by two or more separate disease agents. To the budgerigar breeder, the two most important specific diseases are psittacosis and pullorum, which produce the most common infectious type of diarrhea.

Psittacosis (ornithosis) is caused by a virus which is highly contagious, communicable to humans as well as birds. In humans it attacks adults primarily, but is now curable, one of the few virus diseases that can be cured by a drug. Contrary to general belief it is a rare disease in budgerigars reared in captivity. Pigeons,

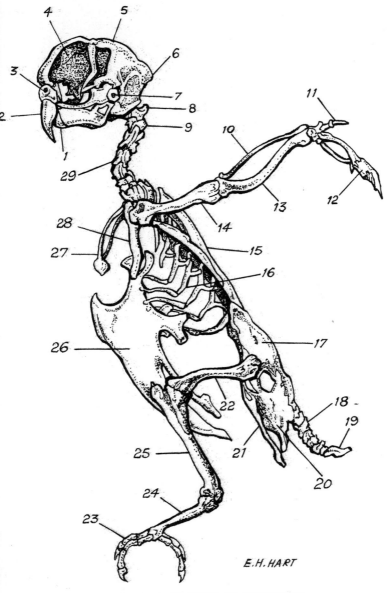

E.H. HART

SKELETAL STRUCTURE OF BUDGERIGAR

1. Mandible 2. Premaxilla 3. Nasal. 4. Eye Socket 5. Skull 6. Occipital 7. Ear
Opening 8. Atlas 9. Axis 10. Radius 11. First Digit 12. Second Digit. 13. Ulna
14. Humerus 15. Scapula 16. Ribs 17. Illium 18. Tail Vertebra 19. Pygostyle
20. Ischium 21. Pubis 22. Femur 23. Toe Bones 24. Metatarsus 25. Tibia.
26. Sternum 27. Clavicle 28. Caracoid 29. Cervical Vertebra.

This Budgerigar lacks badly in spots. It is a German bird
that has been exhibited at a Budgerigar Show in its
native country. Underneath the perch is Budgerigar Score
Card which the judge has used to score and total
the show points of the bird.

On the facing page is a very decorative photo of two
Budgies showing much admired color phases. The Lutino
exhibits the deep, rich yellow color throughout that is wanted
in this species. The other bird is a Normal Violet, a Budgie
of good size and substance, particularly for this
beautiful color phase.

poultry and wild birds, and many species of mammals in great numbers are infected with this virus. Those that survive become carriers and can pass the infection on. The diarrhea accompanying the disease is brownish in color. Treatment consists of the addition of antibiotics to the drinking water (aureomycin, terramycin or sulfonamides). Large doses of vitamin B complex will aid in recovery.

Pullorum is generally considered to be a disease of young birds. The symptoms accompanying the disease are white diarrhea and general depression and debility. The causative agent is the germ *Salmonella pullorum*. Treatment is the same used for psittacosis.

RESPIRATORY DISEASES

There are three main respiratory diseases which affect budgerigars: Infectious coryza, bronchitis and pneumonia. Symptoms are as those accompanying these diseases in humans: Sneezing, watery discharge from nostrils and eye, sinusitis and depression. Pneumonia produces severe shortness of breath, and the bird sits without movement, puffed and with eyes closed. Wheezing is indicative of bronchitis.

The bird should be kept warm and penicillin should be injected into the breast muscles. This drug can also be given in the drinking water, 300,000 units aqueous suspension penicillin in a cupful of drinking water. Aureomycin given orally is also a specific for respiratory diseases. If possible, steam vapor inhalations can bring needed relief. Antibiotics should never be given for more than a five day period, if the patient shows no improvement. The exception to this is in the treatment of psittacosis. The sequel to respiratory infection is quite often chronic asthma.

VARIED NON-INFECTIOUS ILLS

Urinary diseases are frequently associated with a high water intake, liquid feces and an abnormally large passage of urine. Kidney diseases yield to treatment with aureomycin.

Oil duct obstruction is fairly common in budgerigars. If a bird spends more than the normal amount of time working with its beak at the base of the tail, the oil duct is probably plugged up. Part the feathers and you will find a small nipple through which the oil glands discharge. A blackish plug may have formed in the opening. Gently massage the duct and work the foreign material out with the eye end of a needle until the oil can flow readily again.

Tumors should be removed or treated by a veterinarian.

Drastic cere color change in adult budgerigars (female cere color changes to male or in reverse in hens) is often a sign of the degeneration of testes, in the male, or ovary in the female.

DEFICIENCY DISEASES

A bird which lies on its side on the floor of the flight and appears to have a broken leg but does not, is suffering from apoplexy. This disease is often caused by lack of vitamin E. Cortone acetate is the specific used to create a cure. Wheatgerm oil, given as a supplement, can eliminate the cause of apoplexy.

Gout is the most common cause of lameness in budgerigars. The disease is evidenced by swollen and painful hot joints. Treatment consists of a diet rich in greens and vitamin B complex. The affected joints can be painted with tincture of iodine once a week for several weeks.

Though these two ailments are not technically deficiency diseases, they are nevertheless the result of specific dietary lacks and are, therefore, listed here.

Dietary deficiencies can produce many ailments. Rickets, soft beaks and the laying of soft-shelled eggs by a hen are all caused by lack of vitamin D and calcium. Slipped tendons could be due to a lack of magnesium. Eye inflammations and sterility can be produced by the need for a greater intake of vitamin A. Iodine deficiency may cause a goiter.

Coprophagy, or the eating of feces, is also a sign of inadequacy in the diet. The cure consists of supplying wire bottom flights through which the feces will drop out of reach of the birds, and the supplying of an adequate diet.

The obvious cure for all these diseases based upon dietary deficiency is to supply the lacking nutritional elements.

FRENCH MOULT

French moult would seem to be a common term applied to any and all types of feather diseases. There are numerous theories about the causative agent and as many theories anent the transmission of the disease. It is said to be caused by mites in general, or a specific mite in particular, by filth, by overbreeding and

A grand, big violet cock, owned and bred by Dominick Golia, Jr.

Deutscher
Wellensittich-Züchter-Verein (DWV)

Austauschzentrale der Vogelliebhaber
und -Züchter Deutschlands (AZ)

Bewertungskarte

	Punkte	Bemerkungen
Größe, Typus, Kondition und Balance		
Haltung u. Flügelstellung		
Größe u. Form des Kopfes		
Farbe		
Maske und Kehlflecken *)		
(Flügel)zeichnung *)		
Summe		

A pair of hens exhibited in Germany. They show nice deep color and are in good condition, but could use greater depth in bib and smaller, tucked-in beaks.

immaturity of the breeding stock, by a nutritional lack and by bacterial transmission or infection. Many claim the ailment to be congenital or of genetic origin. The clinical picture of French moult is hazy and, as yet, defies definition. In diseases of this nature, coincidence can often mislead the individual to erroneous conclusions, disguised by the cloak of fact, which accounts for the many and divergent theories advanced.

Dr. M. D. S. Armour, the late English budgerigar authority whose integrity, intelligence and experience in the various facets that comprise the budgerigar fancy, was beyond dispute, claimed that French moult was caused by an unidentified arachnid of the fodder mite family. Undoubtedly this mite was present and contributed to the outbreak of French moult which Dr. Armour experienced in his aviaries. In the magazine, Cage Birds, Dr. Armour wrote a scholarly article entitled *French Moult in Budgerigars* in which he described the painstaking scientific approach through which he attempted to track down the causative agent of the disease. To the author, the pertinent sentences in the article which are the keys to the main problem are, "It was when I took up breeding again after the war . . ." and, ". . . all fed with exactly the same quality seed and in the same quantity, all with plenty of sand, cuttlebone and greenfood . . ."

The English stock, necessarily poorly fed during the long, dark war years and, even afterward, not given the benefit of high protein supplementary feeding, could very definitely produce French moult due to the factors involved. These two facts might also be the basic cause for the lack of fertility experienced by some English breeders with certain lines at that same time. Budgerigars can produce crop milk of high biologic quality and produce, overall, a very small percentage of French moult under ordinary and stable environmental conditions. But, when those conditions are inadvertently changed and diets lower in nutritional elements are fed, the inevitable must occur and French moult is the result.

True or typical French moult, as differentiated from other feather diseases, is, in the author's opinion, the result of dietary deficiency coupled with indirect hereditary factors. The author spent several years in experimental research in an attempt to find the answer to the most prevalent form of French moult. Controls were kept as the experiment progressed and every theory formerly

Examples of an advanced form of French moult. Chicks exhibiting the disease to this extent seldom acquire full and healthy feathering when (and if) they reach maturity.

advanced was tested. Nest boxes were deliberately infested with mites and lice, generations of young were hatched and raised in uncleaned nest boxes and filthy breeding cages formerly occupied by French moult parents and chicks. Eggs from parental pairs which were proven French moult producers were switched to and hatched by pairs that by test had never produced French moult, and their eggs hatched by the proven producers. French moult birds were bred together. Recombinations of pairs were tried. Pairs were bred at from four to seven months of age and other pairs allowed to produce as many as eleven clutches in succession and raise from four to eight young in each nest. Among the least important facts evolving from this study was that uncleaned nests and breeding cages are definitely hard to live with.

The sire of these nestlings was a Grey Green Longflight, split to Blue and carrying the sex
linked Lutino factor in a recessive state. The dam was a Cobalt hen. Result: one Lutin
which has to be a hen chick, one Sky Normal (sex not yet determined), and a Dark Gre
Green Longflight male chick split to Blue. Either of the Normal chicks, if cocks, could l
split to the Ino factor, the Blue obviously would be split to Albino.

A cinnamon sky cock bred from top stock and winner of many cinnamon classes.

After considering all the factors involved, the author could find no conclusion which had other than a logical basis in nutritional deficiency affiliated with an hereditary intolerance to specific dietary lack. Considering the phenomenal growth rate of baby budgerigars, the competition between feather and body growth, the fact that proteins, specifically keratin-proteins, which contain the important amino acids, cystine, methionine, glycine and arginine, all of which are the chief components of feathers and extremely necessary for feather formation, are sadly lacking in the basic budgerigar seed diet, coupled with the known fat and protein richness of budgerigar crop milk, the end result of any such experiment could lead only to the same conclusions.

Lack of the ability in parent birds to produce in their crop milk an adequate supply of the keratin proteins and their affiliated amino acids, coupled perhaps with a similar lack in the production of unsaturated fatty acids (vitamin F) will produce French moult in the young. If both parents equally feed the affected young, a change of mates will often stop the incidence of French moult in the nest, indicating that the lack of dietary essentials in the crop milk must be shared by both members of the pair for manifestation of the disease. Since the production of French moult progeny is not common to all budgerigar pairs, even under similar environmental conditions, we can assume that the inability to produce the necessary elements in adequate amount in the crop milk from the basic diet, is inherited as a genetic factor. It would also seem that certain chicks, specifically those from French moult producing parents, possess an hereditary intolerance to the lack of the specific dietary essentials in adequate amount. The disease as such cannot be said to be directly inherited. It has, it seems, a basis in heredity, but will only appear under the stress of adverse nutritional-environmental conditions.

Dipping French moult youngsters in Dett or a Lysol solution will help prevent bacterial infection and thus aid normal feather regrowth. The feeding of a scientifically balanced supplement to the basic diet, rich in proteins and other nutritional elements, and restriction of your feeding parent pairs to two nests a season, and the raising of no more than four chicks per nest, will drastically reduce or completely eliminate the incidence of French moult.

E.H.HART

MUSCULATURE OF THE BUDGERIGAR.

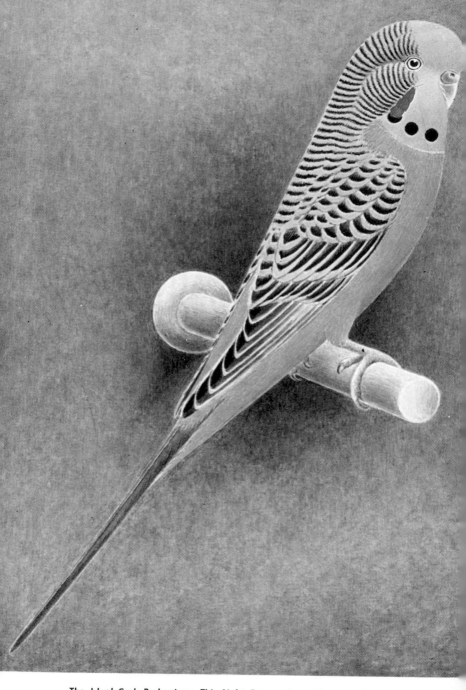

The Ideal Cock Budgerigar. This Light Green mirrors the type that comes closest to the ideal as described in the written standard. From a painting done for the British Budgerigar Society by R. A. Vowles.

cock Light Green Budgerigar of good size and substance with his friend,
Red Factor Canary. Budgerigars, male birds especially, are generally
amiable and therefore are excellent and colorful additions to the
decorative aviary housing a variety of colorful birds.

BROKEN BONES

Leg and wing breaks are not easily set unless the bird is under an anesthetic. The anesthetic dosage is variable in its effect upon budgerigars, even in the hands of experts. It is best then to have breaks or fractures tended by a veterinarian. The primary consideration in setting a broken bone is to have both ends meet properly. For leg breaks, the leg must be held stretched out so that the bone ends are in place. A cast can be made with Johnson's Duo Adhesive. Apply a thick layer to the leg directly from the tube. Press three or four small, flat splinters of wood into the adhesive as it sets, then another thin layer of the cast material and bind around the whole a thin strip of cloth which will adhere to the last layer of adhesive. Leave it on for three weeks.

For wing breaks the broken bone ends must contact when the wing is held in the natural position against the body. Holding it thus, a one-inch strip of gauze is wound around the wing and body, under the uninjured wing to hold the broken member securely in place and form a jacket with the good wing free. Adhesive tape strips will serve to anchor the bandage in place. Do not remove the bandage for three weeks until the break has become firmly healed.

When removing the adhesive cast, first soften the material with vanishing cream. If plaster has been used, vinegar will aid in its removal. Equithesin, an anesthetic recommended for use with birds by Dr. Charles B. Gandel, veterinarian of the Bronx Zoo, is said to be very satisfactory. Equithesin is injected into the breast muscle. The dosage is 2.5 cc. per kg. of body weight.

FIRST AID

In treating wounds, the feathers should be clipped, not pulled, from around the wound and the wound cleansed with peroxide and kept clean. If the wound is deep, an antibiotic such as aureomycin should be given, orally or in the drinking water.

Occasionally a budgerigar will become crop-bound, due to food or foreign substances which it has swallowed, compacting them into a fairly solid mass which the bird cannot pass down to the gizzard. If relief is not given, the mass begins to putrefy and the crop becomes infected. Mineral oil should be forced into the bird's mouth and down into the crop. By gentle kneading of the crop, the oil mixes with and softens the compacted material. Should this fail to bring relief, the bird should be taken to a veterinarian for crop surgery to remove the offending material.

Fright, injuries, exhaustion and chilling can produce shock in a budgerigar. Warmth and quiet will usually bring relief. If the bird has become chilled it should not be given too much heat to begin with. Warming in the hands is good treatment, until the initial signs of chilling has passed. It can then be exposed to greater but gradual heat. Overheating can also be injurious and a bird so stricken should not be cooled too suddenly. Cold drinking water will rapidly reduce the bird's temperature.

A bird which has been poisoned by any of the known vehicles such as paint or unwashed green foods must be given an alkaline physic immediately. Half a dropperful of milk of magnesia will act as a good antidote and aid in ridding the bird's digestive system of the offending poison.

Egg binding must be quickly relieved or a valuable hen might be lost. The egg is normally pushed down the passage, blunt end forward, by constriction behind it. Egg binding occurs when forward propulsion is prevented or the egg is soft-shelled and constriction merely squeezes the egg without pushing it toward the cloaca opening. An unpassed egg in the cloaca prevents the passage of feces and urine. Damming these waste products within the body results in toxemia and death.

To treat the egg-bound hen, hold her in your hand, underparts up, and gently insert a pointed medicine dropper filled with mineral oil between the cloaca wall and the unlaid egg. Squeeze the oil out of the dropper as you encircle the egg. Next, put the hen under heat. This can be done by steaming, putting her in the hospital cage, or putting her on heated sand in a small cage. If any or all of these treatments fail, or if the hen is too far gone when you find her, you must use manual pressure to help her eject the egg. Holding her as before in your hand, with the fingers of the other hand locate the egg and put gentle pressure behind the upper, pointed end, helping her to force it out. The hen will endeavor to help you by muscular spasms. By rhythmic pressure the egg can generally be forced down and through the vent, the membranes covering it. Gradually the membranes will part and the egg will be expelled.

The cinnamon is a sex-linked mutation. Great strides have been made in the breeding of this variety since the first cinnamons, such as the olive green above, appeared. Today cinnamons rank high as show birds.

The second major mutation was the nearly complete elimination of dark (or blue) pigment giving a light yellow or chartreuse color. The fact that there were still traces of dark coloring present gave it the chartreuse shade. From this point, selective breeding resulted in eliminating the chartreuse shade to make a pure yellow or "buttercup." The shade of buttercup was brought about by selection through the use of "modifiers" which are minor variations which can be firmly entrenched in the homozygous state. Modifiers are responsible also for size, type, size of necklace spots, and many other characteristics.

If all else fails, the hen can generally be saved by holding her up, breaking the egg, allowing the egg contents to drain out and then removing the pieces of shell with tweezers. The application of a non-caustic and healing liquid or salve will help prevent infection. The hen should be allowed a period of convalescence in the hospital cage or any small cage where she will be undisturbed, before returning her to the flight cage. Egg binding does not spoil a hen for breeding. Often the hen never again experiences the trials of egg binding. But she should be given a long rest before being bred again.

Where antibiotic medication has been recommended the usual dosage is five milligrams of aureomycin or streptomycin daily. These two antibiotics are specifically named because most of the generalized diseases of budgerigars will yield to them. This medication is most easily given in the bird's drinking water, since even sick birds will consume a limited amount of water daily. Of course, dosing in this manner does not give complete control of the medication intake. For this reason it is best to over-dose by doubling the amount of antibiotics recommended, a process which will do the bird no harm. One-fifth of a 100 milligram capsule dissolved in a teaspoonful of water can be given to the sick bird and all other water removed. After the treated water has been consumed, additional water can be provided and removed during the night. Antibiotic treatment in generalized disease should not be continued for more than five days.

Recently the author, experimenting with his son, Dr. Allan H. Hart, to find a new and more accurate method of administering liquid medication to sick Budgies, found the answer in the use of a hypodermic and a plastic tube of small circumference. Actually, the tubing used was that utilized in hospitals to administer blood or plasma to small children. The medication was drawn up through the needle into the hypodermic barrel in the exact amount. The needle was then removed and the plastic tubing adjusted firmly to the end of the syringe barrel. The tubing was slightly bent. Then, holding the bird in one hand, the tubing was carefully put into the mouth over the tongue then gently pushed down into the crop. The plunger was then slowly depressed until all the medication had flowed from the hypo, through the tube and into the bird's crop. Utilizing this method exact dosage can be given.

Chapter 9

SHOWS AND THE STANDARD

The standard is a written analysis of an exhibition budgerigar. The essence of its combined perfections present to the reader a word picture of a mythical super-budgerigar toward which fanciers must strive. In its entirety the standard disciplines in selection toward an ethical center or objective, which is the breeding of better budgerigars.

STANDARD FOR THE IDEAL BUDGERIGAR (*Courtesy B.S. England*)

CONDITION is essential. If a bird is not in condition, it should never be considered for any award.

TYPE: Gracefully tapered from nape to tip of tail, with approximately straight back line, and a rather deep, nicely curved chest. The bird should be perfectly balanced and should convey the impression of being well and evenly proportioned.

LENGTH: The ideal length is $8\frac{1}{2}$ inches from crown of the head to tip of the tail.

HEAD: Large, round, wide and symmetrical when viewed from any angle; curvature of skull commencing at cere, to lift outward and upward, continuing in one graceful sweep over the top and base of head.

BEAK: Set well into face.

EYES: Bold and bright, positioned well away from front, top and back skull.

NECK: Short and wide, when viewed from either side or front.

WINGS: Well braced, carried just above the cushion of the tail and not crossed. The ideal length of the wing is $3\frac{3}{4}$ inches from the butt to the tip of the longest primary flight.

TAIL: To be straight and tight, with two long tail feathers.

POSITION: Steady on the perch at an angle of 30 degrees from the vertical, looking fearless and natural.

One of the first mutations. The gene for yellow had lost its ability to produce that color. Since the basic green color composed of yellow and blue, deletion of the yellow factor resulted in this early sky blue specimen.

The factor for fallow is autosomal (non-sexed-linked) and is recessive to the normal. Features include brown markings, like those of the cinnamon, a diluted shade of color, and pink eyes. The bird shown is one of the first fallows and a poor specimen.

Proposed ideal opaline hen of the future as interpreted by the author.

MASK AND SPOTS: Mask to be clear, deep and wide, ornamented by six evenly spaced large round throat spots, the outer two being partially covered at the base of the cheek patches, the size of the spots to be in proportion to the rest of the make-up of the bird, as shown in the ideals published by the Budgerigar Society. Spots can be either too big or too small.

LEGS AND FEET: Legs should be straight and strong, with two front and two rear toes and claws firmly gripping perch.

MARKINGS: Wavy markings on cheek, head, neck, back and wings to stand out clearly.

COLOR: Clear and level and of an even shade.

The standard should not be considered rigid and unchangeable. Through mutation, time brings faults and virtues to our budgeri-

Proposed ideal normal cock of the future as interpreted by the author.

Proudly perched upon the spar above the rosette it has won
this sex-linked specimen of the Ino series has made his
owner and breeder proud and happy. The photograph was
taken at a show in Germany.

Three favorite color varieties. At top is a Light Green Opaline, at center is a nice Lutino, and at the bottom is a Normal Light Green cock. All are large exhibition-type birds.

gars which must be recognized and the standard changed to accommodate new values. Since the standard is the yardstick of comparison for judge and breeder, evaluation of new trends must be qualified by not only cosmetic application, but genetic implication as well. Thus, faults which are of an inheritable nature should be penalized more severely than those which are transient.

It is the author's opinion that the standard, as it exists today, is not adequate, particularly in the pictured models of the ideal budgerigars. At the present moment superb budgerigars are being bred and exhibited which are, in many instances, superior to the standard models. In all walks of life the achievement of a higher standard is often so difficult that many attempt to compromise and then come to rationalize the compromise they make.

A standard is of prime necessity, of course, or else the bird breeder or judge, in deciding whether he likes a bird or not, would invoke only his own personal standard. But we who have been guided by the old must not fear the new. We must accept and change to fit new patterns, and to do so requires independent thinking, independently reached.

You will find pictured here a proposed ideal of the future which embodies all the virtues wanted in an exhibition budgerigar but advanced toward the ultimate. Structural balance with feet and legs under the center of balance must be a basic consideration where the top end of the bird becomes so weighty. Greater depth of bib and a corresponding largeness in spot size must balance the amount of head above the cere. The cock bird should display distinctiveness in neck crest, a sexual characteristic wanted in stallions of all species to give that appearance of maleness and nobility. There is an obvious difference in head shape between the sexes. It is even more important for the female to possess slight differences in body shape, in particular greater width and bulk through the pelvic region, for ease in egg laying. Body substance must be sufficient in caliber to match the top end and, to support such depth of bib, the wings will, of necessity, be lower set and possess sufficient length and strength. This ideal budgerigar of the future should have greater length than the present standard calls for.

This ideal is a star to shoot at, a dream that can eventually be achieved and become an actuality through selective breeding and by taking advantage of mutations which direct toward this ideal of the future.

SHOWS

Each year brings larger entries and greater interest in shows as more earnest breeders and enthusiasts realize the vast potential of the exhibition budgerigar. Here is sporting competition in which anyone can indulge with all the anxiety, tenseness and exciting pleasure inherent in such activity. Here one can find release from anxiety from ordinary existence and vocation in personal competition, and can find pride in achievement through a living, breathing entity fashioned by one's hands and knowledge.

Birds are judged by the standard and by a scale of points. The following chart will enable you to check your birds against the point score.

The hope and dream of every Budgerigar breeder is to be able to produce champions and one day to have their owner-breeder Budgie surrounded by winning ribbons.

A pretty girl and a pretty bird. The Budgie is a Harlequin; the Pied coloring and division are recessive.

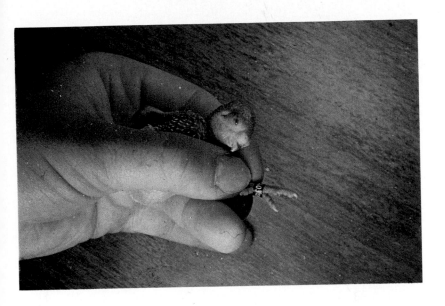

Two steps in the ringing of a chick. Above the front two toes have been pushed through the closed band, the first step in banding. Below the other two (hind) toes, first the larger toe, than the smaller, are being pulled through with the aid of a pointed wooden matchstick. This is not a difficult chore if care is taken and the banding done at the right time.

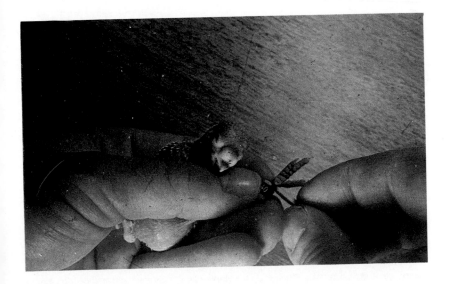

VARIETY	A	B	C	D	E	F
GREEN (Light, Medium, Dark)	30	15	20	15	15	5
BLUE (Sky, Cobalt, Mauve)	30	15	20	15	15	5
VIOLET	30	15	20	15	15	5
YELLOW (Light, Dark, Olive)	30	15	20	35	0	0
WHITE (Light Suffusion)	30	15	20	35	0	0
CLEARWINGS (Blues & Greens) & White, Dark Suffusion	30	15	20	20	0	15
GREYWING (Blues & Greens)	30	15	20	10	10	15
CINNAMON (Blues & Greens)	30	15	20	10	10	15
FALLOWS (Green, Blue, Violet, Grey)	30	15	20	15	15	5
ALBINO & LUTINO	30	15	20	35	0	0
OPALINES (All color varieties)	30	15	20	20*	10	5
GREYS (Light, Medium, Dark)	30	15	20	15	15	5
GREY GREENS	30	15	20	15	15	5
YELLOW FACE	30	15	20	15	15	5
SLATE	30	15	20	15	15	5

*Including clear mantle.

Key to chart.

A—Size, shape, condition and balance
B—Deportment and wing carriage
C—Size and shape of head
D—Color
E—Mask and spots
F—Wing markings

The classes at bird shows are designed primarily to the status of the exhibitor rather than the birds he exhibits. Classes, of course, are plentiful for budgerigars due to the great number of varieties within the breed. But the Intermediate Class, as used in England, would be a happy addition to show lists. It would give the novice exhibitor who has moved out of the novice class, a class in which he can exhibit with more confidence than the Champion Class. We must remember that novice entries frequently make up the bulk of the exhibits and that the novice is the backbone of any fancy and should be encouraged.

Open class winners should always be permitted to compete for Best in Show, though far too often they are not allowed this privilege. Failure to allow Open Class winners to compete for the major prize robs the Best in Show award of much of its value. A budgerigar which achieves a Best in Show placing should definitely be a bird capable of this honor and not just a winning bird from one of the various classes other than the Open Class.

To lend further zest to exhibiting and to give the best budgerigars their just due, a system of diploma or point wins could be devised whereby Best in Show placed birds that have won their award in competition with a set minimum number of entries would be awarded specific recognition in the form of points or diploma awards toward the championship title.* The number of birds in competition could form the basis for point scoring with a maximum number of points that should be awarded at any given show. Individual shows, such as regional shows, could be designated as point or diploma shows. A bird would have had to win points or diplomas in the amount necessary to achieve championship status under a minimum of three different judges at three different shows. Classifications could then be arranged to permit a Specials Only Class composed of budgerigars which have won the Champion title and who would compete against the other winning birds for Best in Show honors. Under this system the Champion Class could eventually be changed to the Bred By Exhibitor Class which is, after all, its true category.

One of the major faults of judging prevalent today is the practice of selecting for the major Best in Show awards from among the birds which have won in their own sections. This would seem, upon cursory examination, to be a logical procedure. Actually, the result of such procedure often eliminates birds worthy of high placement while elevating budgies of less value to the coveted Best in Show placements. In one recent show the author watched a superb class of light greens being judged. The first placed bird went on to Best in Show. The other highly placed birds in this class were automatically eliminated from Best in

---

* Since this book was written the A.B.S. has devised a system for allocating championships and a system of registration. Individual birds will now gain importance, a definite step forward to the time when the classes at bird shows will be geared to fit the exhibit rather than the exhibitor.

Two pet Budgies with their toys. These intelligent little hook
beaks will spend hours with these plastic toys that are
almost as colorful as are they but, of course,
not as cheerfully animated.

Green harlequin (or Danish pied). This is a mature male. In the harlequin variety, as in lutinos, albinos, and fallows, the adult male retains its baby pink cere instead of dark blue. Females of these varieties, like all female buderigars, have brown ceres.

Show competition. The placements for second to fifth Best in Show came from section winners that were greatly inferior to the second to fifth placed birds in the light green class. In this instance all of the five Best in Show birds should have come from the light green class. When a situation such as this occurs, the awarding of the highest honors becomes a farce, breeding value loses its importance, and both novice and experienced breeder become confused.

Frequently the basic reason for exhibiting budgerigars seems to become mislaid in the headlong pursuit for wins and trophies. These rewards are simply tokens of achievement in a much larger pattern. The graded selection of various birds by a competent, unbiased judge enables earnest breeders to weigh and evaluate the products of certain breedings and strains. It aids them also to evaluate their own stock in relation to comparative quality, and gives them an idea which breeding lines can act as correctives to the faults inherent in their own breeding. Here the yardstick of the official standard is used to measure the defects and virtues of individual birds and of the breed as a whole for the edification of both the knowing breeder and the novice.

Here is a typical trophy table at a popular Budgerigar show.

Essentially the judge should be an intermediary between the present and the future, because his decisions shape the trends for better or for poorer. Should these trends lead to undesirable results, there will be deterioration instead of an ever closer approach to breed ideals. The judge is a sounding board, a calculator of degrees of excellence, an instrument for computing worth. With each assignment he can give something of enduring value toward breed improvement. As such, the judge must understand every element of balance and structure, be cognizant of future ideal ambitions within the fancy, and be able to see and evaluate each of those small nuances of quality which establishes the superiority of one budgerigar over another of apparently like excellence. A judge must also possess that special gift that brings clarity and sureness to decision.

The budgerigar judge wields great influence upon the type and quality of the future. Both judge and show lend interest and an important and entertaining reason for the breeder's endeavor.

SHOW PREPARATION

Early training is a "must" if budgerigars are to exhibit their quality to best advantage in the show hall. This training begins in the nursery flight with the attached show cages. Later, promising youngsters should be put up in show cages at various times and placed where human traffic will pass by so they will grow accustomed to the environment they will experience when on exhibition. The breeder and others of his family should stop frequently before the show cage gently blow into the cage with face close to the front, and run their fingers softly across the bars and, as they indulge in this seemingly inane practice, speak quietly to the bird.

If a budgerigar persists in huddling on the floor of the cage it can be gently lifted with a slim stick and placed quietly upon the perch. The stick should be used frequently, stroking the bird and using it to place the bird from one perch to the other, and turning him on the perch. A millet spray hung high above the perch will entice the bird onto the perch and cause him to stretch to reach it, thus teaching him not to huddle over the perch. A piece of cellophane fitted over the inside of the cage front will cure a bird who constantly clings to and crawls around on the bars.

A good yellow-face opaline.

An R.A. Vowles painting of a Budgie. The Budgie's color and form make it an excellent subject for artistic interpretations.

A large Grey cock of excellent substance, tight feather and good head. Both back and front lines are good and flow smoothly. The spots are large, the beak well tucked in, and the bird shows evidence of a nice, full brow. When this Budgie blows his head feathers his head is enormous.

A huge Sky exhibition cock that has done a lot of winning in England. The bird is carrying a bit too much weight at the moment.

A grand, young cinnamon green hen inbred on imported Scotch lines.

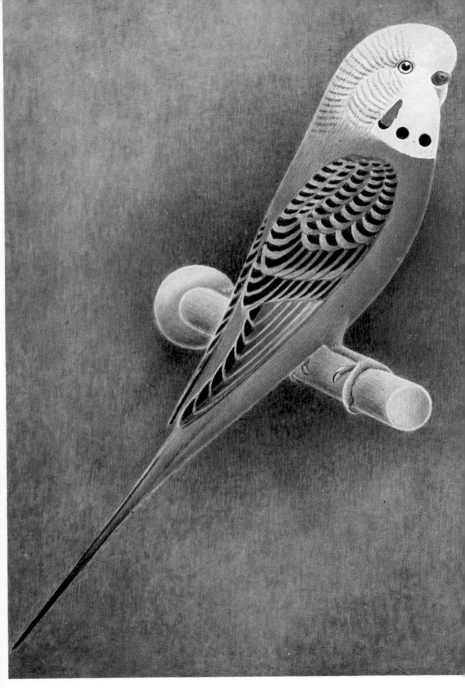

The Ideal Hen Budgerigar as depicted by R. A. Vowles for the English breeders and exhibitors. This is a Violet Opaline. Note specifically the difference in the shape of the skull of the male and female of the species.

This alert-looking male has a nicely formed head.

Chapter 10
MATINGS AND COLOR EXPECTATIONS

Budgerigars have been blessed with a vivid rainbow of glorious color. Crossbreeding and combining these myriad colors results in a fantastic number of matings and expectations. The result for the breeder, and particularly the novice breeder, is confusion. In this chapter the author hopes to simplify this problem and, with the aid of a few tables and in some instances a new approach to the subject, enable the breeder to understand the ramifications involved in factor inheritance, and to determine quickly and easily the results of any given breeding.

We will begin with the assumption that there are but two basic colors—green and blue. All other varieties and blends are but variations produced by modification of the basic green and blue.

Pure light green is the breed foundation color. To create the color green, blue and yellow are combined, therefore the basic green is a combination of blue and yellow in feather pigmentation. The initial departure from this basic color (the first mutation) was the yellow budgerigar. This change in color signified that a color gene mutation had taken place and the factor to produce blue in the pigmentation of the body had been lost. When another mutation occurred affecting the gene responsible for the yellow factor in the basic green so that it failed to produce yellow pigmentation, the result was the mutant blue.

Subsequently, the color genes in other individuals lost their ability to produce complete and full color density and gave us the mutant dilutes, such as greywings, and pastels—yellow, already mentioned, and white. A similar change produced the fallows, and an inhibiting factor gave us the cinnamon. In some mutant individuals the color genes, influenced by modifiers, exhibited two new color depths, medium and dark. Masking, or loss of the ability to produce color, resulted in the albino forms of the green and blue (lutino, albino). The yellow face factor is a return of the basic yellow to the blue series but in a restricted form.

It can be assumed then that mutation in color in the budgerigar is associated with loss or change within the structure of the color genes which inhibits their ability to produce the pure and basic light green form or the secondary recessive light blue (sky). The exception to this is the violet, for in this color mutation we have a genetic additive. To produce the color violet blue and red must be blended. Therefore, the violet is a blue budgerigar to which has been genetically added a new color factor, red. It is the author's opinion, based upon this reasoning, that when and if the long sought for red factor makes its appearance in the pure form in the budgerigar, it will come through the violet mutation. Just as the blue color factor was lost to produce the mutational yellow, and the yellow factor was lost resulting in the blue budgerigar, so may the blue pigmentation be affected and lost in the violet budgerigar to leave only the red factor visible.

BASIC COLOR MATINGS

Green is dominant over all other colors. Grey, violet and dominant pied (clearflight) either partially or wholly dominant, modify the basic green color, they do not dominate it. Blue is recessive to green. The genes which dictate color in the green bird are dominants, those which give the blue color to the blue budgerigar are recessive. A pure green possesses matching pairs of dominant determinants for the color green. A blue budgerigar possesses matching pairs of recessive determinants for the color blue. Both, therefore, are pure breeding for their color within their own color series. The table below lists the basic colors, their suffusion modifiers and their dominant and recessive relationship.

COLOR SUFFUSION RELATIONSHIP

Color Suffusion:	Dominant to:	Recessive to:
Normal Green	All Colors	None
Dilute Green (Greywing Green)	Blue, in all suffusions	Normal Green
Pastel Green (Yellow)	Blue, in all suffusions	Normal Green, Dilute Green

A Clearwing of good substance but lacking in spots, style and head height.

A nice normal but possessing small inside spots a fault difficult to eradicate from a strain.

Normal Blue	All Blue Suffusions	All Green Suffusions
Dilute Blue (Greywing Blue)	Pastel Blue	All Green Suffusions, Normal Blue
Pastel Blue (White)	None	All Green & Blue Suffusions

This healthy pair will definitely produce high quality young.

These pet budgies are not of the highest quality. They exhibit dropping wings, damaged tails, lack of a properly marked necklace   and low foreheads.

Since all green series birds are dominant to all blue series birds, even though normal suffusion is dominant to dilute and pastel, the latter two modified suffusions in the green series exhibit dominance over even normal blue. Thus the mating normal blue × pastel green = 100 per cent normal green/ pastel/blue, progeny.

At the risk of being repetitious the point must be made again that a recessive cannot be split to a dominant, but a dominant color *can* be split to a recessive color. Thus we can have green/blue, but *never* blue/green. A bird can be split for more than one recessive character, for example, green/cinnamon/opaline/blue. This is a fairly simple split, but there are others much more complicated, so that surprises in the nest box from newly bought parent stock can be the rule rather than the exception if the parent stock were purchased from a novice who has a predilection for rares.

In all the matings listed in this chapter the ratios of progeny expectancy are based upon mendelian percentages which, in turn, are based upon the proposed results of many hundreds of matings. You cannot, therefore, expect to recover the exact ratios listed in any given nest or limited number of nests.

DOMINANT AND RECESSIVE DETERMINANTS

The basic genetic table below is exactly similar to the mendelian determinants chart in Chapter 2 and is repeated here, in modified form, for ease in determining results from the breeding of all dominant and recessive colors. By substituting the colors of the birds for the words "dominant" and/or "recessive" according to their category, the results of any combination of basic color breedings can be easily determined. For instance, if you wish to breed a pure green to a pure blue (green × blue) substitute green for "dominant," blue for "recessive." The progeny ratio, as you can readily see, would be 100 per cent green/blue. If the mating you are considering is blue/pastel blue × blue. Since blue is dominant to pastel blue (white) in its own color series, the recovered progeny will show a ratio of 50 per cent blue/pastel blue, 50 per cent blue. Actually, the terms "dominant" and "recessive" are indicative of the kind of relationship that exists between the factor discussed and its normal allele.

DOMINANT AND RECESSIVE MATINGS RATIO

Parents	Progeny
1. Dominant × Dominant	= 100% Dominant
2. Dominant × Dominant/Recessive	= 50% Dominant
	50% Dominant/Recessive
3. Dominant × Recessive	= 100% Dominant/Recessive
4. Dominant/Recessive × Dominant/Recessive	= 25% Dominant
	50% Dominant/Recessive
	25% Recessive
5. Dominant/Recessive × Recessive	= 50% Dominant/Recessive
	50% Recessive
6. Recessive × Recessive	= 100% Recessive

In matings 2 and 4 the resulting progeny which are dominant and dominant split to recessive are visually alike, so their true genetic makeup can only be ascertained by the progeny test (their breeding results).

COLOR INTENSITY MODIFIERS

We next consider color intensity modifiers, commonly called, "the Dark Factor." All budgerigars, regardless of what other genetic factors affect them, are divided into three intensities in all the various suffusions: light, medium and dark, corresponding to light green, dark green and olive green and, in the blue series, to sky, cobalt and mauve. Color intensity is present even when it is inhibited in expression by other factors, as in the lutino and albino. It is also present in pieds, clears, yellows and whites (pastels) where it is also partially masked by other factors but more visible than in the albinos (except in clear).

This intensity modification, the "Dark Factor" mutation, is a partial dominant and cannot be carried in the split form. When the factor is present it produces a visual effect (with the exceptions mentioned):

COLOR INTENSITY MODIFIER RELATIONSHIP

Light green and sky	= No Intensity Modifier (Dark Factor)
Dark green and cobalt	= 1 Intensity Modifier
Olive and mauve	= 2 Intensity Modifiers

Parents: *Progeny:*

No Int.Mod × No Int.Mod = 100% No Int.Mod

No Int.Mod × 1 Int.Mod = 50% No Int.Mod, 50% 1 Int.Mod

No Int. Mod × 2 Int.Mod = 100% 1 Int.Mod

1 Int.Mod × 1 Int.Mod = 25% No Int.Mod, 50% 1 Int.Mod, 25% 2 Int.Mod

1 Int.Mod × 2 Int.Mod = 50% 1 Int.Mod, 50% 2 Int.Mod

2 Int.Mod × 2 Int.Mod = 100% 2 Int.Mod

There exists a genetic linkage between the recessive blue factor and color intensity modification (the dark factor) which results in two types of dark green/blue. The effect of this linkage is segregated into two types, type I and type II (dark green/blue I and dark green/blue II). When the dark factor or color intensity modifier is inherited from the green parent in any given mating which produces dark green/blue progeny, the type I designation is employed (olive × sky).

If the color intensity modifier comes from the blue series bird in the mating, then the dark green/blue progeny are type II (mauve × light green).

If this linkage between the recessive blue and the color intensity modifiers did not exist, the expectations from a dark green/blue mating would show the following progeny color ratio, dark green/blue × skyblue = 25 per cent light green/blue, 25 per cent dark green/blue, 25 per cent skyblue, 25 per cent cobalt. But when we consider the type linkage we see that it drastically changes the ratio of color intensity recovered in the young, as the expectations below correctly show.

TYPE I & TYPE II LINKAGE PROGENY RATIO

Parents: *Progeny:*

Dark Green/Blue-I × Skyblue = 7% Lt. Green/Blue, 43% Dark Green/Blue-I, 43% Skyblue, 7% Cobalt

Dark Green/Blue-II × Skyblue = 43% Lt. Green/Blue, 7% Dark Green/Blue-I, 7% Skyblue, 43% Cobalt

As these results indicate, the dark green/blue I which received its intensity modifier from its green parent passes the modifier down, with greater lavishness to the dark progeny within its own color series. The dark green/blue II, receiving its modifier (dark factor) from the blue parent will pass the dark modifier on to a greater percentage of its blue progeny. It follows that if cobalts or mauves are wanted from a bird, it should be a type II. If dark greens or olives are wanted, the split bird should be of type I inheritance.

COLOR PENETRATION MODIFIERS

The list of budgerigar varieties which carry penetration modifiers include the violet, Australian grey, dominant Dutch pied (clearflight) and yellow face, all mutations from the normal budgerigar. Color penetration modifiers can be inherited as a single factor, displaying partial dominance, or as a double factor exhibiting complete dominance. The dominance of the basic green remains always supreme. Therefore, a budgerigar exhibiting partial or complete dominance associated with penetration modifiers will modify but not dominate the basic green.

Color penetration modifiers act independently but, in the varieties mentioned, can be combined with all other modifiers and linkages.

COLOR PENETRATION FACTOR MODIFIER MATINGS

Parents:	Progeny:
1 Factor Mod. × No Factor Mod. =	50% 1 Factor Mod.,
	50% No Factor Mod.
1 Factor Mod. × 1 Factor Mod. =	25% 2 Factor Mod.
	50% 1 Factor Mod.
	25% No Factor Mod.
1 Factor Mod. × 2 Factor Mod. =	50% 1 Factor Mod.
	50% 2 Factor Mod.
2 Factor Mod. × No Factor Mod. =	100% 1 Factor Mod.
2 Factor Mod. × 2 Factor Mod. =	100% 2 Factor Mod.

VIOLET COLOR INHERITANCE

The violet is one of the most complicated as well as interesting mutations thus far found in budgerigars. Basically the violet is of the recessive blue series, but the red mutation factor which, when merged with cobalt gives us the visual violet, also brings with it

233

color penetration modifiers in either single or double factor. Since, to produce visual violets we must breed as if for the production of cobalts, with the addition of the red factor, of course, we must also take into consideration color intensity modifiers. The violet, like its less vivid brother, the cobalt, cannot be bred pure from a pair of its own color since each parent bird will only possess a single intensity modifier (dark factor) and, therefore, together they will produce all three intensities in the blue series, plus visual, sky and mauve violet.

Theoretically the best matings to produce visual violets are:

1. Sky Violet × Mauve   = 100% Visual Violet
   (2 factor   (No factor   (1 factor pen. mod.)
   pen. mod.)   pen. mod.)

2. Mauve Violet × Sky   = 100% Visual Violet
   (2 factor   (No factor   (1 factor pen. mod.)
   pen. mod.)   pen. mod.)

Since two-factor violets and, especially, two-factor sky violets or mauve violets are almost as rare as the extinct Dodo, (the factor number can only be proven by the progeny test), it is best to consider all violets, visual, sky or mauve, as single factor birds.

The best matings to produce visual violets from single factor penetration modifier budgerigars are:

1. Sky Violet × Mauve   =50% Cobalt, 50% Visual Violet
   (1 factor)   (No factor)   (1 factor)

2. Mauve Violet × Sky   = 50% Cobalt, 50% Visual Violet
   (1 factor)   (No factor)   (1 factor)

To complicate matters further most sky violets and mauve violets must be "test mated" before we can be certain that they carry the violet modifier and are not simply cobalt or normal mauve. For this reason it is recommended, particularly to the novice breeder, that one of the breeding team used to produce violets should itself be a visual violet.

When one of the parent birds is a visual violet the best and least complicated matings to produce more visual violets are:

1. Visual Violet × Sky   = Sky, Sky Violet, Cobalt, Visual Violet
2. Visual Violet × Mauve   = Mauve, Mauve Violet, Cobalt, Visual
                                             Violet

Both these matings will produce 50 per cent one intensity modifier (single dark factor) budgerigars, of which approximately 25 per cent will be cobalts and 25 per cent visual violets.

An excellent, winning light green cock. This color variety is dominant to all other colors.

CLEARWING COLOR INHERITANCE

The clearwing mutation can be bred in either green or blue series birds and is recessive to all colors except dilute and pastel. It can, therefore, be carried in the recessive or split state, by any variety other than pastel. The linkage with greywing (dilute) will be discussed later. It is listed in most mating tables as possessing one or two factors for clearwing inheritance. With the number of factors which the breeder has to consider this only leads to unnecessary confusion. Actually a clearwing is either pure for the character or it is impure and, therefore, split to pastel.

The table charting expectations from dominant and recessive heritage can be handily used for clearwing inheritance. Simply change "dominant" to read "clearwing," "recessive" to "pastel." The split forms, "dominant/recessive" become "clearwing/pastel." The same table can be employed when clearwing is crossed to normal but, since clearwing is recessive to normal, it becomes the "recessive" in the table and the "normal" becomes the "dominant."

With the introduction of the sex-linked opaline into the clearwing variety the combined form, opaline clearwing, or "self" opaline is produced.

FULL BODY COLOR GREYWING INHERITANCE

The interaction of the color genes of the clearwing variety and the greywing (dilute) leads to an apparent balance of chromatic color which results in the full body color greywing. The body color of this variety assumes the color richness and depth of the deepest clearwing suffusion, about 90 per cent of the normal color depth, instead of the 50 per cent color depth of the ordinary greywing (dilute). The wings, back, neck, head striations and throat spots retain the dilute grey, often a shade darker than the ordinary greywing.

Quite frequently both clearwings and greywings are split to pastel, but test matings are not necessary to determine if they are so split, since the matings listed below give the answer via progeny color ratio. The term "pure" is employed to designate a clearwing or greywing which is not split to pastel.

1. Pure Clearwing × Pure Greywing = 100% Full Body Color Greywing

2. Clearwing/Pastel × Pure Greywing = 50% Clearwing/Pastel
   50% F.B.C.* Greywing

3. Pure Clearwing × Greywing/Pastel = 50% Clearwing/Pastel
   50% F.B.C. Greywing

4. Clearwing/Pastel × Greywing/Pastel = 25% Clearwing/Pastel
   25% Greywing/Pastel
   25% F.B.C. Greywing
   25% Pastel

---

*F.B.C. = Full Body Color.

These Yellow-green budgies have small heads and crossing wings, making them not at all good for exhibition.

An almost perfectly marked White Flighted Blue Pied. This bird is of the normal pattern and of excellent type. He was twice winner, in England, at the National and Club Shows. An almost perfectly marked White Flighted Pied Opaline, is shown below. This was also a fine bird, its major fault being the lack of pure white tail feathers.

If a full body color greywing is employed as one (or both) of the parents, the best matings are:

1. F.B.C. Greywing × Pure Clearwing = 50% F.B.C. Greywing
   50% Pure Clearwing

2. F.B.C. Greywing ×
   F.B.C. Greywing = 50% F.B.C. Greywing
   25% Pure Clearwing
   25% Pure Greywing

A full body color greywing can never be split to pastel regardless of parental source. It exhibits a unique blending of two different varieties, the clearwing and the greywing (dilute).

SEX-LINKAGE

Budgerigar varieties that follow the pattern of genetic sex linkage include the cinnamon, opaline, lutino and albino. The latter two varieties are the albino forms of the green and blue series birds respectively. To indicate the albinism in both series collectively, the last three letters of the variety names are borrowed and an albino in either the green or blue series is given the designation, INO.

Sex-linkage is a recessive characteristic which results in a loss of black pigmentation in wings and striations, and a corresponding lessening of color suffusion value on the body in the hypomorph cinnamon, a change in color extension and pattern in the opaline and a lack of pigmentation accompanied by the typical albino eye in the INO.

The major difference between the non-sex-linked recessive and the sex-linked recessive lies in the fact that a hen cannot be split for a sex-linked recessive but a cock can. The female budgerigar must visibly display the evidence of the sex-linked character in order to possess it at all and be capable of passing the linkage on to her progeny. A male budgerigar need not display the sex-linked character but can carry it in the split state and so be capable of stamping it upon a percentage of his get. The INO factor can successfully mask the visible manifestation of a sex-linked character, but this is the only exception.

A cock can be split to more than one sex-linked characteristic just as he can be split to more than one non-sex-linked recessive. In the following table the name of any sex-linked variety can be sub-

This proud-looking male, with its nicely spotted necklace, correctly formed wings and strong feet, is definitely a winner.

stituted for the word "sex-linked" to arrive at a specific conclusion.

SEX-LINKED INHERITANCE

Cock		Hen	Progeny
1. S-L*	X	S-L	Both sexes S-L
2. S-L	X	Non-S-L	Cocks—Non-S-L/S-L
			Hens—S-L
3. Non-S-L	X	S-L	Cocks—Non-S-L/S-L
			Hens—Non-S-L
4. Non-S-L/S-L	X	S-L	Cocks—Non-S-L/S-L and S-L
			Hens—Non-S-L and S-L
5. Non-S-L/S-L	X	Non-S-L	Cocks—Non-S-L/S-L and Non-S-L
			Hens—Non-S-L and S-L

*S-L = Sex-Linked.

When using this table remember that when dealing with two sex-linked characters in the same bird or mating, one variety only must be used to replace the key word "Sex-Linked" in the table. For instance, if the male parent is cinnamon and the female, opaline, though both are genetically sex-linked varieties, the characters which produce them individually are influenced by different genetic factors in the X chromosomes so their progeny ratio must be deciphered individually from the above table. Such sex-linked combinations can be easily worked out through study of the table.

Recombination or crossover in sex-linkage which gives us the combined forms such as opaline cinnamon, is the result of a chance gene recombination in the sex chromosomes. The greater the distance between the genes which influence the separate sex-linked varieties, the greater will be the chance of crossover, or recombination to produce the combined form.

The study, understanding and usage of the various genetic factors that give such great variety to our budgerigars is fascinating. But whatever colors, modified or pure, you choose to breed or experiment with, remember that type and quality in form is paramount. The old horseman's adage that a good horse cannot be a bad color is almost as pertinent when applied to budgerigars as it is to horses, with a modicum of reserve.

A fine, young Pied Hen. Note her cere, encrusted and dark brown, indicating that she is ready for the breeding cage where she will, if bred to the right cock, produce promising offspring.

Chapter 11

TRAINING THE PET BUDGERIGAR

The breeding of stock specifically for the pet market has long been a lucrative part of the budgie fancy. As many show breeders will tell you, a good percentage of the chicks hatched each year from top quality parents do not come up to the breeder's expectations. These scrubs are usually sold as pets.

With few exceptions, most cage birds of other species are merely ornamental or kept, as are canaries, for their song. The beauty in color, form and stance of the budgie is hard to equal, so it can qualify as a pet simply from the angle of eye appeal. But, besides its obvious beauty, the budgie can be trained to become a *real* pet, to come to the owner's call, to perch upon his shoulder or finger, to perform various interesting tricks, and even to talk. Add to this the fact that this little bird is clean in its habits and more hardy than most other birds, and you have the perfect pet.

Most breeders of top quality, expensive show stock, give little heed to the pet area. But it has its own importance and value, for the pet budgie brings a great deal of happiness to many people. Shut-ins, handicapped people, youngsters, and those who live lonely lives, find companionship and pleasure in their little pet budgie.

The heavier bodied, more phlegmatic and quieter birds of imported breeding are apt to make better pets than the so-called "American" birds. Birds bred from English stock are less likely to be biters and, due to their larger, heavier bodies, not given to such quick aerial gyrations.

Training the budgie as a pet is not a very difficult job. It is, of course, essential that the bird be a healthy one, and a typical representative of the species and the color variety you select. Your task will be made much easier if you acquire a very young chick, one that has been out of the nest box only a few days but who is cracking seeds and eating without trouble and no longer needs auxiliary feeding from the parent birds. Most youngsters of this tender age will almost immediately become finger tame, the first step in training the pet bird.

It is advisable to put the youngster immediately into the cage which is to be his home. Keep the cage in a stationary place away from drafts and household turmoil, and give the little fellow a chance to settle in and become accustomed to his new surroundings. Make sure the cage has open seed cups and keep them constantly filled with seed. The water cup must always be filled with fresh water. At this tender age we cannot be sure that the chick will locate and eat the seeds in the cups, so supply a layer of seeds on the floor of the cage for his convenience until you are sure that he is picking and eating seeds from the cups.

When near the bird or working around him, such as filling his seed and water cups, speak to him in a soothing tone and be sure that your movements are fairly slow and deliberate. Never make quick, jerky movements with your hands or you may frighten him. And always try to keep your hands on a level with, or lower than, the bird, for budgies are afraid of movements above or over their heads.

FINGER TRAINING

Do not wait too long before you begin the actual training. After a day and night in his new quarters the training of your pet budgie can begin. Wait until he is on the perch, then gently and slowly insert your hand through the cage door, into the cage and slowly move your fingers toward the bird so as not to alarm him. Stroke his breast gently with your finger, at the same time speaking to him in a soothing voice, repeating the name you have chosen for him over and over again.

Budgies love to have their necks and the back of their heads scratched. By doing this you impart a pleasurable sensation to the young bird which he will begin to associate with the presence of your hand and so lose all fear of you. Frequently the chick will step up on your hand from the perch of his own accord. If he does, the first obstacle in training will be overcome. If he doesn't, press your finger gently against his lower breast where the bird's thighs join the body. The pressure of your finger will gradually push him back off balance, and he will step up onto your finger by necessity. When he does, give him a command such as UP. After a few tries he will automatically step from the perch onto your finger when you command UP, and he will then be finger trained within the limits of his cage.

The next step is to remove him from the cage while he is perching on your finger. Remember to move your hand slowly. It is best to attempt this new part of his training at night for, if he becomes frightened, or senses freedom and flies from your hand, he can be easily captured again. Mark the spot where he lands and then turn out the lights to recapture him, since a budgie will never attempt to fly in the darkness.

CLIPPING THE WINGS

Many people who have trained budgies advocate clipping the primary wing feathers so that the bird cannot fly and will, therefore, after one or two abortive attempts, remain on your finger when free of the cage. Whether to clip or not to clip depends on the individual bird. If he insists upon flying from your finger and after landing will not allow you to approach without taking off again in flight, his wings should be clipped. But, quite often, after the initial flight or two, the bird will allow you to approach and will then hop back again onto your finger. If he does, he will be tractable and it is not necessary to clip his wings. Remember: always use the same command, in the same vocal tone, so that the bird will recognize it and understand its meaning.

Once the budgie has been completely finger trained and will come flying to his finger perch upon command, he can be given the run of the house at specific times. You will find him lighting upon your shoulder or your head while you work around the house, for he becomes used to your company and likes to be close to you. The little tyke will fly to the table while you eat and steal food from your plate, a cute custom that sometimes ends in disaster. A pet budgie plopping into a plate of hot soup can become a quick case for a veterinarian. Or, a pet jumping onto a piece of chocolate cream pie, and then zipping onto your head when your involuntary scream frightens him, can wreck havoc with the most carefully done coiffure.

A playpen for your pet, made especially for the amusements of this species, will provide both pet and owner with hours of fun. Your budgie will learn many cute tricks by himself when allowed freedom in a playpen with its assortment of interesting objects.

If you contemplate advanced training for your pet, or a series of tricks similar to those performed by birds displayed on TV programs, it is best to begin your training with a T-stick, rather than your finger. The stick is used to move the bird from one object to another on which he is going to perform his tricks, and he is seldom, if ever, asked to perch on the finger or the hand.

TEACHING TO TALK

Teaching your pet to talk is not difficult, but it does take patience and time. Remember that he does not recognize words or words in sequence; he merely recognizes sounds and has the ability to reproduce those sounds in sequence. *Repetition* is the basis of successfully teaching a budgie to speak. Begin with easy sounds, the bird's name and a word or two, such as: HELLO, PETEY. Repeat it over and over again when there is no other sound or activity in the immediate neighborhood to distract your pupil. A bird generally learns more quickly when the voice of the tutor is in the higher registers. For this reason women and children make better tutors than do men. You must be extremely patient and repeat the simple words over, time and time again, even though it may seem futile because the bird doesn't utter a sound that can be even loosely interpreted as being close to the simple words you are trying to teach him to say. It may take weeks or months, but after a while you will hear the bird making strange sounds that are not the ordinary budgie vocal sounds. Soon after this occurs the bird will repeat the words you have been teaching him, generally mixed with a string of garbled noise.

Once he has mastered the first few words he will advance much more quickly, and, given time, will become a veritable chatterbox, much to the owner's delight. He will also pick up and repeat words that have not been deliberately taught him, if they are repeated frequently within the home. And, since he merely mimics without understanding, his speech can be a wild mixture of all the words and phrases he has learned.

The vocabulary of some birds, particularly those which have been owned and tutored patiently by women who live alone and grow close to their pets, can border on the unbelievable. The author has heard budgies recite rhyme after nursery rhyme, sing songs, mimic trains and other odd sounds, including a dog barking, tell jokes and humorous stories, and all in such a devastatingly cute and humorous way that it is difficult to imagine that the bird is actually speaking or that it is merely mimicking without understanding.

To own and train a pet budgie to the limit of his capacity to learn can be a great source of satisfaction and one can take pride in the accomplishment. Considering all that can be done with this little immigrant from Australia it is no wonder that they are the delight and pride of many homes throughout the world, and that they are more sought after as pets than any other creature that mankind names in this category.

On the left is a good quality Clearwing, nice stance and good head. The bib could be deeper. On the right is a nice Opaline showing the large spots this variety is noted for. The tail should be in line with the body.

Chapter 12
THE FUTURE

The future of our hobby is inevitably hidden by the veil of time. We do not know what that time to come will bring. Yet, this we do know; in the final analysis the future of the fancy rests in the hands of those who breed and exhibit the beautiful budgerigar *today*. To you the future flings a challenge, and you must meet that challenge.

Ours is a young fancy when compared to the many hobbies man enjoys. And, like all things in their springtime of growth, much that is wonderful lies ahead. We who form the ranks of the fancy must look to other fields of similar endeavor and make ourselves aware of the myriad forms that have arisen and been adopted and, by breeding skill, fashioned into new breeds within a species. Take cognizance of the many breeds of dogs developed from the basic canine form. Note the varied breeds of fancy and specialized pigeons that have been derived, through mutation and development, from a single, early type. These are but two examples of type diversity achieved within a species structure; two of the many to be found in other areas of live stock breeding. From these sources we borrow the key to the future of our own hobby.

As time passes more varied and diverse mutations will appear in the budgerigar. Cherish those departures from the norm, the crested birds, the long flight and any other bizarre mutant that may appear in your nest boxes. From them can be developed new variations, new branches of the fancy, that will eventually lead to specialized clubs and standards, bigger and more interesting shows, and a much broader breed basis as the fancy expands and flows into new channels.

New theories, new concepts and discoveries are constantly being made in the many fields of scientific endeavor. Future research will uncover new roads to Psittacinae nutrition and medicine. Geneticists probe ever deeper into the why of being, delving into

A massive light green cock of Scottish ancestry. A multiple Best-in-Show winner and a prepotent stud.

the core of life itself, and giving us, if we look for them, new answers to our breeding problems. We must face this future with open and inquiring minds, learn to understand and accept new ideas and avoid harking back blindly to the incomplete knowledge of the past. We must take the fresh tools made available to us in the future and use them well.

This is the future; a time when yesterday's miracles become tomorrow's accepted facts. So remember this; beyond the last word I have written lie the many new words the future will write, continuing and improving on what you have read here; words that will help you, as the years pass, to breed better and better budgerigars.

The End

It is difficult to entirely eliminate the scientific terminology which is an integral part of the study of genetics. Certain terms and symbols have specific definition and are consistently used for clarity. The following definitions will aid the lay reader to better understand these terms and symbols. They appear in order of importance and you are urged to learn them before reading the text.

1. GENE (noun; adj. *genotypic*). A single unit of inheritance, (Mendel's "Determiners"); a microscopic part of a chromosome.

2. CHROMOSOMES (noun; adj. *autosomal*). Small microscopic bodies within the cells of all living things. When division of cells begins the chromosomes appear as short strings of beads or rods.

3. DOMINANT (adj.). A trait or character that is seen. Indicates that a trait contributed by one parent conceals that from the other parent. For example, Green is dominant over blue.

4. RECESSIVE (adj.). A trait or character that is concealed by a like dominant character. Exception: when no dominant is present and recessive genes pair for a certain trait. For example, blue/white × blue/white will produce the Mendelian ratio of 25% whites. Paired recessives = Visibility.

5. FACTOR (noun). A simple Mendelian trait; may be considered synonymous with gene.

6. HETEROZYGOUS (adj.). Possessing contrasting genes (or allelomorphs). Where dominant and recessive genes are both present for any trait or traits.

7. HOMOZYGOUS (adj.). Pure for a given trait, or possessing matched genes for that trait. The opposite of heterozygous. (Thus inbred strains are said to be homozygous, and outcrossed budgies to be heterozygous. Degree must be substantiated.)

8. GENOTYPE (noun; adj. *genotypic*). The hereditary composition of an individual. The sum total of every budgerigar's dominant and recessive traits.

9. PHENOTYPE (noun; adj. *phenotypic*). The external appearance of an individual. The outward manifestation of all dominant genetic material (or double recessive. See *Recessive*).

10. ALLELOMORPHS (noun; adj. *allelomorphic*). Genes, factors, traits or types which segregate as alternatives. Contrasting gene pattern.

11. ALLELE (noun). A gene, factor, trait, which differs from its sister gene. See *Allelomorph*.

12. AUTOSOMES (noun; adj. *autosomal*). Paired, ordinary chromosomes, similar in both sexes, as differentiated from the sex chromosomes.

13. CROSSING-OVER (noun). An exchange of inheritance factors or genes between related chromosomes.

14. HYPOSTASIS (noun; adj. *hypostatic*). The masking of the effect of a factor by the effect of another factor, not an allelomorph. For example, the masking of the dominant pied head patch by the opaline factor.

15. EPISTASIS (noun; adj. *epistatic*). Similar to hypostasis. Like dominance but epistasis occurs between factors not alternative or allelomorphic.

16. ♂ . Indicates a cock or male. The symbol represents the shield and spear of Mars, the God of war.

17. ♀ . Indicates a hen or female. This symbol represents the mirror of the Goddess of love, Venus.

18. ✕. Means "with", "between", etc. A mating between any male and female.

19. F_1. Represents the first filial generation. The chicks, progeny, or "get" produced from any specific mating.

20. F_2. Is the symbol used to denote the second filial generation, that is, the progeny, or young, produced from a mating of a cock and hen from the F_1 breeding above.

21. GET. Chicks or offspring.

This is a typical pet budgie. Although not of the most perfect quality, it is not too badly proportioned.

INDEX